20 BEST

USED CARS
VANS AND
TRUCKS
1986 - 1991

1992 Edition

Jack Doo
Author

Standard Book Number: 87759-402-3

Copyright © 1992
by Edmund Publications Corporation

ALL RIGHTS RESERVED

Printed in the United States of America

ABOUT THE AUTHOR

Author Jack Doo, one of the nation's leading auto writers, has kept pace with the changing automotive world as a nationally syndicated columnist and as an editor for The Modesto Bee newspaper.

Doo, 37, is a six-time winner of the prestigious Moto Award, presented by the National Automotive Journalism Association. He is the author of The Ultimate Owner's Manual, The Front-Wheel Driving High-Performance Advantage and Japanese Exotic Cars.

Doo, who has chalked up racing victories in Formula Ford and Showroom Stock, does his own maintenance on his seven-car fleet. He lives on a farm in Turlock, CA with his wife Cathy and sons Brandon, 6, and Barrett, 1.

TABLE OF CONTENTS

INTRODUCTION
AND BUYER'S CHECKLIST

The right used car can be the very best automotive bargain. The wrong used car can be the worst nightmare.

The 20 Best Used Cars, Trucks and Vans can help make sure your used car is a dream come true and not a nightmare.

This book was extensively researched to uncover the best of the best in used cars, trucks and vans. The recommendations and extremely comprehensive information focus on specific years, models and options. Pricing is based on 1992 Edmund's Used Car data.

In all cases, the very best year of a particular model is singled out. Consideration is given to year-by-year improvements, refinements and value.

For example, in the category of Best Used Sports Car Under $15,000, the 1987 Porsche 944S was selected out of the three-model 944 lineup. The 944S got the nod because its all-new 16-valve cylinder head gives it nearly the performance of the much more expensive 944 Turbo at a price just slightly higher than the base eight-valve 944.

With the Cadillac Allante, the Best Sports Coupe Under $20,000, the 1989 model is the best buy — make sure to avoid the '87 and '88 models — as the '89's new, more powerful 4.5-liter V-8 transforms the Allante from an also-ran to a world class performer.

Looking for a full-size pickup? Then read the facts on why the '88 Chevrolet C1500 is the one to buy.

The right used car can be the best automotive bargain because a car is new only once. When those wheels roll off the showroom floor, the odometer goes up and the value goes down.

Depreciation. The bane of new car buyers, but the salvation of used car buyers.

It is estimated that a typical new car loses up to 25 percent of its value each of its first two years, making a $16,000 new car worth only $9,000 after two years.

Letting the original buyer pay for the depreciation is an age-old strategy practiced by used car buyers.

Other used car benefits are lower insurance costs and a "de-bugged" car

— most mechanical problems showed up for the original owner and were repaired under the warranty.

BUYER CHECKLIST

No matter where or how the right used car is located, the procedures for separating it from a car lot of wrong cars is the same. The following is a used car inspection checklist:

Check

Mileage

The average car is driven between 10,000 and 15,000 miles annually. Depending on the type of driving, don't eliminate from consideration a relatively high-mileage car or automatically purchase a low-mile vehicle.

A high-mileage car that has been used as a commuter vehicle can be a great buy. Price guides call for a deduction for high mileage, but a car with 60,000 easy highway miles is about equivalent in wear to a car with 30,000 miles of normal usage.

A car with low miles may have been subjected to short trips and city driving which are much harder on an engine. Short hauls do not allow the engine to warm-up enough to burn off corrosive internal condensation.

A tip off to a short trip vehicle is a rear muffler that is rusting, burned out or has been prematurely replaced. The muffler, with damage much easier to spot than an engine's internals, would have been eaten away by the corrosive condensation.

Odometers can be rolled back. A tampered odometer can be difficult to detect, but a buyer should look for numerals misaligned on the odometer and brake and accelerator pedals and a driver's seat with excessive wear for the mileage. Also look for service stickers on the door posts and air filter that have the mileage for when service was performed.

Contact the previous owners about the mileage. California and other states for a fee of about $5 supply information on the vehicle's former owners.

A new car dealership of the same make can call up the vehicle identification number (VIN) and report its warranty and recall history and the mileage when work was completed. Dealerships are willing to do this because they want any needed warranty or recall work done in their shop.

Check

☐

Body and Chassis

Ask if the vehicle has been in an accident. Make sure the exterior is clean and straight.

Previous body and frame damage can be spotted by checking to see if any body panels are slightly off in color and if there is any overspray inside the hood and fenders.

Gaps between the body and doors, trunk and hood should be uniform. Look for rust, especially around the base of the windshield, the bottom of the doors and rear fenders.

Overall, the exterior should be clean. A late-model vehicle should not have needed a paint job.

Check

☐

Interior

The interior of a well-cared for vehicle should be like new with little wear on the door liners and seat covers.

Make sure the driver's seat is not internally broken down and sagging from over use. Look under any seat covers or floor mats for any excess wear.

Check

☐

Engine

The engine should start instantly and idle smoothly. Rev the engine and check for blue smoke, a sign of excess oil consumption. The inside end of the exhaust pipe should be off-white in color, indicating clean burning. A black, sooty deposit is found in an oil burner.

Place a newspaper on the ground under the engine, let the engine idle for five minutes and check for leaks. Check the condition of the hoses and belts.

Transmission or Transaxle

Check ☐

Check for leaks and fluid level. Look out for burnt-smelling automatic transmission fluid and a dark brown color. Good automatic transmission fluid should be pink in color.

With a front-wheel-drive vehicle, examine the constant-velocity joint boots for rips or tears.

Any "clunk" when the drive is engaged could signal worn universal joints or drive shaft. The rear end differential should operate quietly.

Cooling System

Check ☐

Check for leakage around the water pump. The coolant should be relatively clean, showing regular service. Inspect the front passenger floor area for any heater core leakage. Heater core leakage can also show up as a fogged windshield.

Electrical System

Check ☐

Check battery strength in turning over engine. Does the voltage or amp meter show the alternator is charging?

Accessories

Check ☐

Try out every accessory — radio, windshield wipers, heater, air conditioner, defogger, power windows, power door locks, etc. — and make sure they work.

The cost of repairing a power window unit or replacing an air conditioning compressor can be the difference from a good buy and a costly mistake.

Check

☐

Brake system

Check the warning lights. The brake pedal should be firm under pressure. Taking off one front wheel will give a good idea of brake condition and remaining life. Vehicle should stop in a straight line.

Check

☐

Steering System

Check for excess free play in the steering. Inspect wear of front tires for possible alignment problems. Check the power steering unit belt for cracks and any leaks.

Make sure the steering wheel is square and pointed straight when the front tires are in the straightaway position. A crooked steering wheel can be the tip-off to a misaligned front end or an improper alignment.

Check

☐

Suspension System

Jack one front corner off the ground and shake tire assembly to check for excess wear and loose components. Check shock absorbers and struts for leakage.

Test the shocks and struts by bouncing vigorously on each corner, stopping and then counting how many times the vehicles bounces up and down before stopping. If it takes more than two complete cycles, the shocks or struts are worn.

As with your other inspections, worn shocks don't necessarily eliminate the vehicle from your selection process, but the cost of repairs should be factored in and used as a bargaining point.

Check

☐

Tires

Check for tread depth, matching brands and sizes and any obvious damage or uneven wear.

Make sure the car has a good spare tire. If the spare has been used and is worn unevenly, this could be caused by a poorly aligned front suspension.

Vehicles sold by dealers are required to have a spare tire and a working jack and lug wrench. With a private seller don't take a chance, inspect the spare, jack and lug wrench.

Check

☐

Exhaust System

Look and listen for any leakage and exhaust smoke when the engine is running. Check the mufflers, especially the rearmost unit, for any rusted or burned out spots.

Check

☐

Test Drive

Test drive a used car as you would a new car. Drive it and test it in the fashion in which you plan to use it.

Take the car over a variety of roads. Turn off the radio and listen for noises from the engine, brakes, transmission or steering.

The steering should be positive and the body and suspension solid. The car should start instantly and be able to be driven smoothly away — immediately.

Drive the car over a clear, long stretch of road at least 50 mph, then release the gas pedal sharply, letting the car slow under engine compression without braking. Next accelerate hard. Blue smoke out the exhaust under these conditions could mean the engine's valves or rings are marginal and expensive repairs will soon be called for.

Another quick test is a stress test recommended by the Consumer Federation of America.

The CFA test is for automatic transmission vehicles only. With the engine at idle, the air conditioner is turned on maximum, the headlights set on high beam and the radio and every other electrical accessory turned on, the vehicle is placed in drive with the brake on and the steering wheel is turned lock-to-lock in both directions.

A car in good mechanical shape will continue to run smoothly as the stress test is conducted. If the power steering squeals, the engine surges or dies, there are potential problems needing further examination.

Check

Final Inspection

If a car you like passes this used car inspection checklist and test drive, take it to a qualified mechanic or an independent diagnostic center.

Investing a little money in a diagnostic check can save you from making a $10,000 mistake.

A private seller of a car might split the cost of the diagnosis with you. If you buy the car, it was a cheap cost to close the deal. If you don't buy the vehicle, the seller can use the diagnostic report as a selling tool for the next potential buyer.

BEST COMPACT SEDAN
Price Range: Under $5,000

The goal is to find an inexpensive, used, compact sedan that will continue to provide troublefree, reliable and economical transportation.

THE CONTENDERS*

	WHOLESALE	RETAIL
1986 Honda Accord	$3,050	$3,950
1987 Toyota Camry	$3,850	$4,750
1987 Volkswagen Jetta GL	$3,450	$4,350

*Prices of Contenders are base prices which may vary in range from those of the winning model.

The Winner

1987 VOLKSWAGEN JETTA GL

Selecting the best compact sedan under $5,000 is a tough job. Five thousand dollars just doesn't buy what it use to.

However, this is one of the most relevant categories in our list of the 20 best used cars. The $5,000 cap fits the needs of entry-level buyers, students and families needing a second or third car.

The key to the best car in this price range is its dependability, durability and reliability after the new wears off. For less than $5,000 you can expect the used vehicle to have rolled up more than 50,000 miles and possibly upwards of 75,000 miles. Reasonable expectations after buying such a car is to drive it for at least another 50,000-plus trouble-free miles.

Many cars are good when the showroom shine is still bright, however after 50,000 miles — when the new wears off — they can rapidly go downhill.

The '87 Volkswagen Jetta GL is our pick for the best compact sedan under $5,000 because of its durability, ease of service, and low-cost replacement parts.

Such traits are nothing new for Volkswagen. The German automaker, which recently built its 60 millionth vehicle, built its reputation with vehicles that were inexpensive to operate, easy to service, reliable and long lasting.

The Volkswagen Beetle, which amazingly is still being produced in Mexico, established the Volkswagen tradition of building simple, but well-engineered designs that lend themselves to do-it-yourself service and repairs. The Bug became a legend in America because it was easy on gas and easy to service and repair.

With the Jetta, the basic concept is the same. With common tools and a Robert Bentley repair manual, an owner that can follow directions can keep a Jetta running for a long time.

For example, the transversal engine layout is very straightforward. The four spark plugs are in plain view and easy to change. You can easily place both hands around the oil filter. Access to other major components such as the alternator, waterpump and starter is good. Disc brake pads and rotors have been designed for ease of replacement. And the list goes on.

If you prefer not to do your own service and repairs, the lack of complexity of the Jetta helps keep labor charges down at repair shops. For example, at the same $50 per hour rate, new car dealerships quoted $140 to change the timing belt of a Jetta, compared to $400 for a Toyota Camry.

The Jetta and its near twin, the Golf Hatchback are true world cars and are produced in global plants that include Germany and Mexico. No matter the location of the plant, all Volkswagens must meet a worldwide standard.

This global mass production of the Jetta and Golf, which share mechanical components, results in a tremendous economy of scale when it comes to purchasing factory and aftermarket parts. For example, front disc brake rotors for a Jetta can be purchased from an aftermarket firm for less than $20 each. Other major components can be found at similar bargain prices.

The parts themselves and the Jetta in general are very tough and durable. No other car in its class has been as thoroughly abused and tested to the limit and beyond. Jetta-Golf components and powertrains have survived the ultimate testing — the real life testing on a race track.

The Rabbit/Bilstein Cup and later the Golf/Bilstein Cup were racing series that pitted very slightly modified Volkswagens in a national racing series. The only modifications allowed were the addition of safety equipment and Bilstein gas struts and coil springs. The engine, transmission and brakes were all showroom stock and proved to be bulletproof. It was rare to ever see a Bilstein racer not finish a race because of mechanical failure.

Wrapped around the proven powertrain and mechanical package is a wedge-shaped, five-passenger sedan with a huge 16.6-cubic feet trunk. Jetta variations include the two- and four-door standard Jetta, the luxury four-door GL and the high-performance Jetta GLI, which costs about $500 to $600 more than the GL.

In a recent insurance survey, the Jetta was the only compact car to be in the top ten for accident survival.

The durability of Jettas has not escaped notice by the industry. According to the July, 1991 N.A.D.A. Central Edition study of resale value, from 1986 to present, the Jetta GL retains more of its original value at resale than any model BMW, Mazda or Nissan.

Size, Comfort and Style

German engineering has made the Jetta much bigger on the inside than it appears on the outside. In fact, the Jetta has more interior volume than a BMW 5-Series sedan. The Jetta can seat up to five passengers, but is most comfortable with four passengers. The spacious trunk can easily swallow luggage for all passengers.

Driver comfort is excellent with the Jetta. The wedge-shaped body with its sloping hood affords great visibility, as does the car's generous green house.

The Jetta is an excellent fit for nearly every driver. Short stature drivers will appreciate the height-adjustable, fully reclining front bucket seats. All four-door models have height-adjustable upper seatbelt anchors for the front seat passengers to improve wearer comfort.

The Jetta design is a typical form-follows-function, understated German design. The Jetta's wind-cheating shape is the result of extensive development in Volkswagen's Wolfsburg, Germany wind tunnel. The Jetta has a drag coefficient of 0.36 — excellent for the relatively tall and practical shape.

Aerodynamic halogen headlights, front spoiler, dual remote-control outside mirrors and tinted glass are standard on all Jettas. Black wheelhouse flares and rocker panel trim and blacked-out treatment between taillights distinguish the Jetta GL and GLI.

ENGINE AND DRIVETRAIN

The Jetta base engine displaces 1.8-liters and is rated at 85 horsepower at 5,250 rpm and 96 foot-pounds of torque at 3,000 rpm. The overhead cam engine is mated to a five-speed manual transmission, with a three-speed automatic optional. Top speed with either transmission is 106 mph.

The base engine is understressed and has a race-proven history. The same basic engine with its cast-iron block, forged steel crankshaft with five main bearings and aluminum head is used in the Volkswagen Corrado in supercharged form and pumps out 158 horsepower — nearly double the base Jetta unit.

The base engine is well matched to the gearbox and pushes the Jetta to 0-60 mph in 10.5 seconds. The combination also clicks for 26 miles per gallon city and 34 mpg highway, according to EPA testing.

The high-performance Jetta GLI has a more powerful 102 horsepower high-output version of the 1.8 engine. The GLI accelerates from 0-60 mph in 9.5 seconds and has a top speed of 116 mph.

Both engines feature hydraulic valve lifters that require no periodic adjustments.

HANDLING

As proven in the Volkswagen/Bilstein Cup racing series, the Jetta and Golf are excellent handling vehicles. A Jetta has also won its class in the Sports Car Club of America's National Solo II Championships.

The key to the Jetta's impressive ride and handling is the independent rear suspension and V-profile torsion beam axle with integral trailing arms. The V-profile axle and track-correcting bushings provide much of the same effect as the Weissach rear axle of the Porsche 928 S4 or the "Neutral Steer" axle of the BMW 750IL — a pair of $75,000-plus cars.

The front suspension is designed with a negative roll radius that forces the car to brake and track straight, even when a tire is flat.

The handling of the Jetta is very good for the average driver and great for the better driver that can take advantage of the car's sporting capabilities.

Those capabilities are even higher with the sporty GLI. Identified by its understated red accent trim on bumpers and side molding, the GLI has larger 14-inch light-alloy wheels with low-profile 185/60R14 high-performance radials. The GLI package also includes a larger rear stabilizer bar, power-assisted, four-wheel disc brakes and power-assisted quick ratio rack-and-pinion steering.

Brakes

Power front disc and rear drum brakes are standard on all models. The high-performance GLI model includes power-assisted, four-wheel disc brakes and larger tires to further improve the stopping power. Later model Jettas are also available with an optional anti-lock braking system that prevents tires locking and maintains steering control during panic stop situations.

Ride Quality

The Jetta's sophisticated four-wheel independent suspension gives it what Volkswagen has been calling Fahrvergnugen — crisp, taut handling and the solid feel of a German-engineered car.

Part of the solid feel comes from a separate subframe that carries the engine and transaxle and is bolted to the unitized body. Many vehicles in the compact class have the powertrain attached directly to the unit body. The body structure of the Jetta also features a rigidly-welded safety cell that encompasses the passenger compartment. The reinforced design adds to the structural integrity of the Jetta.

The Jetta suspension boasts generous wheel travel and a combination of relatively soft springs and stabilizer bars. This setup allows for a good ride, while still allowing the Jetta to stick to the road around tight curves.

INTERIOR

The interior of the Jetta was redesigned in 1987, with more luxurious upholstery fabric on the Jetta and Jetta GL. The base-model features upgraded tweed-cloth interior and cloth front headrests. Velour-covered rear headrests were added to the '87 Jetta GL along with new design velour upholstery.

Opting for the high-performance GLI dresses up the interior with a leather-wrapped steering wheel, gearshift knob and shift lever boot.

The dash instruments — analog speedometer, tachometer, water temperature and fuel gauges — are placed directly in front of the driver. Rocker switches for the lights and other functions, along with the radio, are mounted high within the driver's peripheral vision and are within easy reach.

The interior also includes a glove box and handy storage bins for odd items at the center console and the lower portion of each front door.

The GLI features an on-board multi-function trip computer. At the press of a button located at the tip of the windshield wiper stalk, the computer instantly displays engine oil or ambient air temperature, elapse time of trip, miles traveled, average speed, average miles per gallon and time of day. A two-position memory switch, also located on the wiper stalk, allows the driver to keep the total trip information plus data on trip segments.

Interior options include an extremely powerful air conditioning system, sliding steel sunroof with air deflector, passive safety belt system, height adjustable driver's seat, cruise control, automatic transmission, power steering, power windows, central locking system and electrically operated and heated outside mirrors.

SUMMARY

The Volkswagen Jetta offers a rugged and reliable sedan that is the size of most subcompacts, but with an EPA-rated interior volume of a compact.

The efficient package provides excellent fuel economy and spirited performance and great handling. The Jetta continues the Volkswagen tradition of being inexpensive to own with its straightforward mechanical design and low-cost replacement parts. Like the Volkswagen Beetle, the Jetta is also known for its long-life potential and sturdy powertrain.

1987 VOLKSWAGEN JETTA GL

ASSETS
Proven engine
Huge trunk
Powerful air conditioning
Good handling

DEBITS
Radios are popular with car thieves.
Insurance surcharge

HOW THE RUNNERS-UP PLACED
FOLLOWING THE VOLKSWAGEN JETTA GL

2nd PLACE...Honda Accord
Premium price for used models, suspension tuned for soft ride, not handling.
3rd PLACE...Toyota Camry
Costs go up after the new wears off. Parts cost particularly high.

A CLOSER LOOK AT THE 1987 VOLKSWAGEN JETTA GL

SPECIFICATIONS: Front engine, front-wheel drive, two-
                                   or four-door sedan. Options include
                                   the high-performance GLI version.

ENGINE:	Four cylinder
DISPLACEMENT:	1.8 liter
HORSEPOWER:	85 @ 5,250 RPM
TORQUE:	96 foot-pounds @ 3,000 RPM
INDUCTION SYSTEM:	CIS fuel injection
RECOMMENDED FUEL:	Unleaded regular
DRIVETRAIN:	Five speed manual, three-speed automatic
FRONT SUSPENSION:	Independent with MacPherson struts, 18mm stabilizer bar, coil springs
REAR SUSPENSION:	Independent torsion beam axle, coil springs
STEERING TYPE:	Rack-and-pinion
TURNING CIRCLE (CURB-TO-CURB):	34.4 feet
BRAKE TYPE:	Power-assisted front disc/rear drum
TIRE TYPE AND SIZE:	P175/70R13
WHEELBASE:	97.3 in.
LENGTH:	171.7 in.
WIDTH:	66.1 in.
HEIGHT:	55.7 in.
CURB WEIGHT:	2,330 pounds
TRUNK CARGO VOLUME:	16.6-cubic feet
ACCELERATION, 0-60 MPH:	10.5 seconds
FUEL CONSUMPTION:	26-34 miles per gallon

BEST LUXURY COMPACT SEDAN
Price Range: Under $15,000

A luxury compact sedan is the entry-level into the finer things in life. The target vehicle must have all the features luxury class vehicles are known for in a compact package, with driving pleasure and performance to match.

THE CONTENDERS*	WHOLESALE	RETAIL
1988 BMW 325i	$11,775	$13,600
1986 Mercedes-Benz 190E	$9,850	$11,350
1989 Toyota Cressida	$11,575	$13,375

*Prices of Contenders are base prices which may vary in range from those of the winning model.

The Winner

1988 BMW 325i

A compact luxury sedan is just that — all the power features, amenities and opulent surroundings of a luxury car downsized into a compact car. That sounds like an easy formula to follow, but it is very difficult to compose and orchestrate all the individual pieces and players into one fine-sounding concert.

The three contenders in the best used luxury compact sedan under $15,000 are all top-rated, but one — the four-door BMW — gets the nod for its blend of smoothness, six-cylinder performance, road feel and handling, and overall refinement. The 325i is also one of the most imitated autos in the industry, but it's hard to beat the original.

That's because BMW has had a headstart building quality-made and high-performing small sports sedans. The legendary 1600 and 2002 Series debuted nearly three decades ago. Since that time, BMW has been a moving target for its competitors, always improving and refining its cars.

The popular four-cylinder 320i Series debuted in 1977 and the German automaker took the compact sedan to new levels with the 1984 six-cylinder, 325 sports sedan. The original 325 used BMW's "eta" 2.7-liter, 121-horsepower engine that was engineered for low-revving efficiency, good torque and low fuel consumption.

The various BMW components soon began to come together to create a leading compact luxury sedan. A four-door 3-Series was introduced in 1985 and in '87 BMW made its high-performance, 168-horsepower, 2.5-liter six available on the small BMW.

The 325i, BMW's first true luxury compact sedan, debuted in 1987 and as in BMW tradition, was further refined in 1988.

The 168-horsepower six-cylinder engine gives the 325i excellent power to go along with BMW's legendary reputation for building the smoothest engines in the world. With 164-foot pounds of torque at 4,300 rpm, the powerplant has excellent low-end power and can launch the 2,850-pound 325i to 60 miles per hour from a standing start in just 8.5 seconds. The "six" operates on unleaded regular gas and is EPA rated for both manual and automatic transmissions at 18 miles per gallon city and 23 mpg highway.

On the luxury side, the 325i's standard amenities include an acoustically matched premium sound system with power amplifier, eight speakers and custom-contoured graphic equalizer. Also standard are an electric tilt/slide sunroof, leather seating, electronic temperature control air conditioning, anti-theft AM/FM stereo with cassette, power windows, rear window defroster, a nine-function onboard computer and BMW's exclusive Service Interval Indicator, which custom-tailors the maintenance schedule to the owner's own driving style and operating conditions.

Special twin-tube, gas-pressurized shock absorbers are designed for comfort and performance. An anti-lock braking system is also standard.

One option other compact luxury cars cannot match is a 325i Convertible. The 325i Convertible is the only open-top model BMW offers. The Convertible, which maintains full four-passenger seating, has a manually operated top, utilizing gas struts to assist the raising and lowering.

The two-door 325is is the sports model in the three model 325i lineup. The 325is uses the same 2.5-liter engine as the 325i and Convertible, but differs from its running mates with firmer suspension tuning and larger front and rear anti-roll bars. The 325is can be identified by its front airdam with integrated foglights, a small rear spoiler, three-spoke, leather-rim steering wheels, leather upholstery and front sports seats with more prominent side bolsters for extra lateral support. The "is" costs about $500 to $600 more than the "i".

All 325 models come standard with a five-speed manual transmission or an optional four-speed automatic overdrive.

BMW recently released the all-new 1992 325i, the latest generation of 3-Series. The new model brings the 325i to a new high with more interior room and performance. However, the '92 model's $30,000 sticker makes an '88 325i at less than $15,000 look very attractive.

Size, Comfort and Style

The 3-Series was ideal to spin off a four-door model. Small BMW's have long been known for their roomy interiors, made possible by their tall, glass-surrounded cockpit. The top section also does not slope down until well past the rear seats, giving it an abundance of rear seat headroom.

This straightforward, two-box body design is balanced over a 101.2-inch wheelbase and spread over an overall length of 175.6 inches. From the driver's seat, the 325i appears even smaller, due to the excellent visibility and relatively high seating that gives a commanding view of the road over the hood and at every corner.

The 325i earns its luxury car designation with a long list of standard creature comfort features that include an acoustically matched premium sound system with power amplifier, eight speakers and custom-contoured graphic equalizer. Also included are an electric tilt/slide sunroof, leather seating, electronic temperature control air conditioning, anti-theft AM/FM stereo with cassette, power windows, rear window defroster, a nine-function onboard computer, and the famous BMW drop-down tool kit in the trunklid.

The only available options are the four-speed automatic transmission, limited-slip differential, and metallic paint.

In the styling department, the BMW 325i has been the leader that many automakers have envied, borrowed from and copied. The 3-Series with its "yuppie" association set the standards for exterior and interior styling for this class of vehicle. BMW has done this with a design that has remained true to its "form follows function" philosophy. BMW also has been able to maintain the family look of its cars. BMW's, even without spotting the twin kidney grilles, are instantly recognized.

ENGINE AND DRIVETRAIN

The 2.5-liter BMW six was introduced in 1987 and created by modifying the existing 2.7-liter, low-revving eta unit with a shorter stroke. The result is a slightly smaller engine that loves to rev to its 6,400 rpm redline and produces 168 horsepower — up from the 121 of the original eta. The 2.5-liter unit is rated at 164 foot-pounds of torque at 4,300 rpm.

The single-overhead cam, inline six, which runs on regular unleaded gasoline, is topped off with a free-breathing aluminum crossflow cylinder head. The engine parameters are monitored by BMW's Digital Motor Electronics (DME), which instantly adjust the engine electronics and fuel injection.

The DME system features an adaptive electronic idle control, which even automatically adjusts to reduce friction as the engine is broken in. Its

Lambda-sensor emission-control loop is adaptive, for better running over a wider range of operating conditions such as large changes in elevations. The sophisticated engine management system results in the 325i having both a top speed of 130 mph and an EPA highway rating of 23 miles per gallon.

The potent engine is teamed to a standard Getrag five-speed manual transmission. A ZF four-speed automatic is optional and has a torque converter and torque-converter lockup clutch. The ZF unit operates with little loss of performance. According to BMW, the automatic 325i is just one tenth of a second slower to 60 miles per hour than a manual transmission car. The automatic also has the identical fuel mileage ratings for the manual transmission.

Both the manual and automatic transmission share a 3.73:1 final drive ratio. A limited-slip differential is standard on the 325is and optional on the 325i.

HANDLING

BMW has built its reputation on the incredible handling and road feel of its vehicles. BMW's philosophy in vehicle dynamics is "the driver is a fully functional part of the car itself, the human part of the equation which completes the car's mechanical system."

The 325i is no different. When driving the 325i, it becomes an extension of the driver. The steering is alive with feedback on the condition of the road surface and input from the workings of the suspension and tires.

Much of the steering wheel feedback is from the power-assisted rack-and-pinion steering system and the sophisticated front suspension that features positive offset steering geometry. The tried and true front suspension is independent with MacPherson struts, sickle-shaped lower A-arms, coil springs, gas-pressurized shock absorbers and an anti-roll bar. The rear suspension features semi-trailing arms, coil springs, gas-pressurized shock absorbers and an anti-roll bar.

The 325i is relatively softly suspended for a good comfortable ride. When cornered hard, the car's body rolls and then takes, sets and follows the intended course.

Brakes

Power front and rear disc brakes are standard. The front and rear discs measure 10.2 inches, with the front units ventilated. Also standard is an anti-lock braking system. The anti-locking system prevents the tires from locking in a panic stop or slippery conditions. This reduces stopping distances and maintains steering control. The excellent brake system is completed with low-profile P195/65VR14 high-performance radial tires.

Ride Quality

BMW engineers were able to achieve both a soft, comfortable ride and high-performance control with the 325i. The key is the development of twin-tube, gas-pressurized shock absorbers. The twin-tube units feature double valving — in the piston and at the connection between the two tubes — which provides non-linear dampening that gives the engineers more latitude in tailoring shock action. On the 325i this means relatively soft dampening on small bumps, but progressively firmer dampening as the going and surface get rougher.

Other components contributing to the excellent ride quality are the strong unitized steel body, sophisticated independent suspension and the 65-Series tires.

INTERIOR

The interior of the 325i is laid out with the driver the as No. 1 priority. The dash wraps around in front of the driver. The electronic speedometer and tachometer are the dominant gauges that are seen through the top half of the four-spoke steering wheel. The dash's center section is canted toward the driver and includes the controls for the anti-theft stereo and levers and knobs for the electronic temperature control air conditioning.

BMW's nine-function onboard trip computer registers trip fuel economy and instantaneous mileage among its functions. The BMW Service Interval Indicator signals when maintenance is required by monitoring the number of cold starts and trip lengths. Vehicles making short trips and not thoroughly warming up require servicing sooner.

The fully reclining front seats also have adjustments for height. The seating areas are leather on the 325i and the carpeting material is velour. BMW claims the rear seat can hold three passengers, but it is much better for two passengers, split by the folding center armrest.

SUMMARY

The 1988 BMW 325i is not only an entry-level vehicle in the world of luxury cars, but is also an entry-level model into the world of BMW. The German-made cars have a huge following and customer loyalty. This was earned by manufacturing "Ultimate Driving Machines" that drive and handle like extensions of their drivers.

The 325i has the heritage and the famous BMW six-cylinder engine to back up its performance claims. The list of standard features rivals any conventional luxury tourer. If the 325i does not meet a buyer's exact requirements, the 3-Series line-up also includes the 325is two-door sports sedan and 325i Convertible. All are well equipped and come standard with anti-lock brakes. All are true BMW's.

1988 BMW 325i

ASSETS
Responsive engine
Anti-lock brakes
Convertible model
refined

DEBITS
Factory service and parts are expensive

HOW THE RUNNERS-UP PLACED
FOLLOWING THE BMW 325i
2nd PLACE...1989 Toyota Cressida

Smooth 190 horsepower six powers this Toyota flagship. The BMW 325i has more head-turning style, sport handling and is a recognized status vehicle.

3rd PLACE... 1986 Mercedes-Benz 190E

The 190E matches the BMW 325i in status and styling, but its four-cylinder engine falls short in power and smoothness to the six-cylinder competition.

A CLOSER LOOK AT THE 1988 BMW 325i

SPECIFICATIONS:	Front engine, rear-wheel drive, four-door sedan.
ENGINE:	Inline six-cylinder
DISPLACEMENT:	2.5 liter
HORSEPOWER:	168 @ 5,800 RPM
TORQUE:	164 foot-pounds @ 4,300 RPM
INDUCTION SYSTEM:	Electronic multiport fuel injection
RECOMMENDED FUEL:	Unleaded regular
DRIVETRAIN:	Five-speed manual
FRONT SUSPENSION:	Independent with coil springs, gas-pressurized shock absorbers, anti-roll bar
REAR SUSPENSION:	Independent with coil springs, gas-pressurized shock absorbers, anti-roll bar
STEERING TYPE:	Power assisted rack-and-pinion
TURNING CIRCLE (CURB-TO-CURB):	32.2 feet
BRAKE TYPE:	Power-assisted front and rear discs with anti-lock braking system
TIRE TYPE AND SIZE:	P195/65R14
WHEELBASE:	101.2 in.
LENGTH:	175.6 in.
WIDTH:	64.8 in.
HEIGHT:	54.3. in.
CURB WEIGHT:	2,850 pounds
TRUNK CARGO VOLUME:	14.3-cubic feet
ACCELERATION, 0-60 MPH:	8.5 seconds
FUEL CONSUMPTION:	18-23 miles per gallon

BEST LUXURY SEDAN
Price Range: Under $20,000

The essence here is an outstanding ride as well as quiet and comfort for up to six passengers. Surrounding them are opulent features and a host of powered creature comforts.

THE CONTENDERS*	WHOLESALE	RETAIL
1990 Cadillac Seville	$15,200	$17,850
1990 Lincoln Continental Signature Series	$15,925	$18,575
1986 Mercedes-Benz 300E	$15,150	$17,800

*Prices of Contenders are base prices which may vary in range from those of the winning model.

The Winner

1990 LINCOLN CONTINENTAL SIGNATURE SERIES

In the race for the Best Luxury Sedan Under $20,000 the victory goes not to the swiftest, but to the vehicle with the most comfort, quiet ride and lavish accommodations.

That automobile is the 1990 Lincoln Continental Signature Series. Introduced in the 1988 model year, the all-new Continental was a major revamping of the luxury car concept. To begin with, most luxury cars featured rear-wheel drive. Power through the front wheels had basically been limited to subcompact and compact economy cars — not luxury cruisers.

Ford challenged this thinking by making the Continental the largest production front-wheel-drive car ever. With a 109-inch wheelbase and an overall length of 205.1 inches, the '88 Continental is larger than the rear-wheel-drive model it replaces.

By exploiting the front-wheel-drive layout's inherent space-efficiency, Ford engineers were able to package the Continental with a spacious interior that is limousine-like in size. Many automakers may make that claim, but the Continental is a true six-passenger car.

The huge 19.1-cubic foot trunk can handle the luggage for those six passengers. The carpeted trunk has a practical shape and can be opened from a remote trunk release in the glove box. With the Continental Signature Series, you do not have to slam the trunk lid down to close it. With the power trunk closer you just move the trunk lid down until it meets resistance and then a motor pulls the lid closed. Slick.

Ford did not stop with just building a space-efficient luxury car, the automaker went on to make the Continental its most technologically advanced vehicle.

The Continental, which was selected in *Car and Driver* magazine's "Ten Best" list, has microprocessor-controlled front and rear air springs with automatic front-to-rear and side-to-side leveling, speed-sensitive, variable-assist power rack-and-pinion steering, power four-wheel disc brakes with an anti-lock braking system, electronic instrument panel, driver's side and passenger side airbags.

Standard equipment includes nearly every power luxury feature available, including automatic climate control, heated remote control mirrors, power driver's seat, tilt steering wheel, AM/FM stereo with cassette, trip computer, power windows and door locks, and fingertip cruise control.

The Signature Series adds geometric-spoke alloy wheels, dual-illuminated visor mirrors, power decklid pulldown, automatic headlight control convenience group, power passenger seat, Ford premium JBL sound system, memory driver seat and dual lumbar support.

Buyers living in harsh winter climates should seek out a Continental with the Insta-clear option. The windshield heater can clear a windshield of snow and ice within minutes.

The one knock on the Continental has been with its straight line acceleration. There is only so much a 3.8-liter V-6 rated at 140 horsepower can do with 3,623 pounds. However, with its low drag coefficient of 0.34 and responsive four-speed automatic transmission, the Continental makes the most of all those horses. While the Continental can go from 0-60 in approximately ten seconds, what is more important — especially for a luxury car — is its ability to cruise quietly and effortlessly at highway speeds and even at triple digits. Once the car is off the mark, power and response are very good.

If you need more acceleration, opt for the 1991 Continental which has an improved dual-exhaust system and other engine refinements for an additional 20 horsepower — 160 total. It will cost $2,500 to $3,500 more than the 1990.

The high-tech V-6, four-speed overdrive automatic transmission and clean aerodynamics also make the Continental amazingly fuel efficient. With an EPA fuel economy rating of 17 miles per gallon city and 24 mpg highway, the Continental is very likely the most fuel efficient large car.

On real roads, the Continental can even top its EPA numbers. At a steady 65 mph, the car's very accurate trip computer shows the big Lincoln covers 27 miles for every gallon of gasoline.

Size, Comfort and Style

In size, the high-tech Continental is very traditional — big on the outside and big on the inside. The Continental interior is actually larger than a conventional sedan of the same 109-inch wheelbase and 205.1-inch length. That's because the front-wheel-drive layout with its space-saving transversal-mounted engine, allows a larger portion of the vehicle to be devoted to the passengers.

The Continental is one of the few automobiles that treats rear-seat passengers as well as those in the front. Up to six passengers — three each in the front and back seats — can enjoy the Continental's limousine-like legroom. Shoulder room also is excellent and three adults — not just children or dogs — can truly sit comfortably across each of the seats. Since there is no driveline to the rear axle with the front-wheel-drive layout, the very shallow center tunnel enhances the comfort of the middle passenger in both seats.

Comfort can also be measured in decibels. The Continental excels in this area as one of the quietest cars on the road. The low-drag aerodynamics makes for little wind noise at speed and the powertrain is well isolated and insulated.

The Continental's styling blends both the new and the traditional. The new is represented by the rounded "aero" look and the large greenhouse area of the passenger compartment. The traditional is represented by the elegant and understated lines, the 205.1-inch length, long-hood and long-trunk proportions. The interior styling has a very traditional American luxury car look with its over-stuffed seats that would not be out of place in the front room of a home.

ENGINE AND DRIVETRAIN

There is only one engine available on the Continental. The 3.8-liter V-6 has undergone continued refinement since it was introduced in 1988. In 1989 it received sequential multi-port fuel injection and roller valve lifters. The 1990 version is rated at 140 horsepower at 3,800 rpm and 225 foot-pounds of torque at 3,000 rpm.

The 1991 version, with further refinements and an improved dual exhaust system pumps out 160 horsepower at 4,400 rpm. Note that the '91's 20 additional horsepower achieved 600 rpm higher than the '90 unit. With its wider and more useable powerband, the 140-horsepower unit really does not give much away to the more powerful engine in normal driving and in the all important middle range of power.

The four-speed automatic transmission shifts smoothly. The overdrive top gear can be locked out, for such times as when driving in the hills, by placing it in drive. This prevents the transmission from "hunting" between fourth and third.

The slick shifting transmission plays a large role in getting all of the Continental's 140 horses to the road. When in overdrive it quickly downshifts to boost acceleration. Ford also aided acceleration by going with a 3.37:1 final drive ratio, compared to the car's initial 3.19:1.

HANDLING

The Continental comes standard with a very sophisticated suspension that features microprocessor-controlled front and rear air springs. The unit instantly adjusts for front-to-rear and side-to-side leveling. The quick-acting system keeps the Continental level and balanced. The air suspension is complemented by nitrogen gas-pressurized hydraulic struts and a 0.75-inch diameter front stabilizer bar and a rear 0.71-inch rear stabilizer bar. The air suspension system is similar to the optional air suspension available on the Lexus LS400.

However, the Continental's air suspension is programmed on the "soft" side, more for ride comfort than performance. This programming shows up when putting the Continental through its paces. Even with its sophisticated air suspension, it corners much like a heavy, rear-wheel-drive luxury sedan, safely, but with heavy understeer. The hardware is there, but the software is lacking.

What is not lacking is the excellent traction the Continental has with its front-wheel-drive and P205/70R15 radial tires. With the majority of its weight over the driving tires, the Continental is sure-footed in slippery road conditions.

The Continental's steering system uses a speed-sensitive, variable-assist power rack-and-pinion. The system varies the amount of power steering assist based on vehicle speed. At low speeds, as when making parking maneuvers, the assist is greatest. The amount of power assist then declines as the vehicle speed increases for better road and steering feel. The 38.4 feet turning circle is much shorter than with similar sized cars.

Brakes

The power front and rear disc brakes ensure the Continental can be quickly brought down from speed. The diameter of the front and rear disc rotors is ten inches. An anti-lock braking system is standard. The ABS system eliminates wheel lock-up and maintains steering control during severe braking applications regardless of the road surface or conditions. From 60 miles per hour, the Continental stops in 150 feet. Overall, the brakes receive an excellent rating.

Ride Quality

The sophisticated suspension features computer-controlled front and rear air springs which are programmed for a traditional American luxury car ride. This old school of thought results in a very soft ride that is good over smooth highways.

The supple suspension has enough wheel-travel and control to handle potholes and large bumps. The air springs and its automatic level control keep the ride height constant and the car level, regardless of the number of passengers or luggage load.

The excellent ride quality is achieved with some sacrifice to handling. Ford engineers opted for a luxury car, not a sports sedan.

INTERIOR

The interior is where the Continental stands out. The interior has the room and quality that you would expect in a limousine. The over-stuffed front and rear bench seats are upholstered in leather. The front seats have built-in inflatable lumbar support and numerous power-assisted adjustments. The Signature Series has power recline for both front seats.

The front split-bench seat has dual center-mounted armrests that also serve as the center passenger's backrest. The center tunnel is low, thanks to front-wheel drive, and gives center passengers good legroom. Head, shoulder and leg room are excellent.

The large and sharp digital displays can easily be seen through the top portion of the four-spoke steering wheel. However, the key readouts, such as the oil pressure and engine temperature, must be called up one at a time by pushing a button.

The driver's door armrest houses many of the controls for the car's power accessories, such as outside mirrors, windows and door locks, and with just a little practice can easily be operated without taking your eyes off the road.

Possibly the most important interior feature is an airbag for both the driver and front passenger. The Continental in 1990 was one of the very few cars to offer the dual passive restraints.

SUMMARY

If you were shopping for a sports sedan, the Lincoln Continental would not be the car for you. However, the Continental is the clear choice for the used luxury car under $20,000. Luxury ride, surroundings and styling are what the Continental is all about. No other car has the unique blend of ride comfort, spacious interior, silence, fuel efficiency and safety.

In addition to optimizing the interior package, the Continental's front-wheel drive also ensures excellent traction on slippery surfaces and conditions.

Selecting the Signature Series adds many desirable features — including power decklid pulldown and the Ford JBL sound system — to the Continental's already long list of opulent standard equipment.

1990 LINCOLN CONTINENTAL SIGNATURE SERIES

ASSETS
Anti-lock brakes
Large interior
Excellent fuel economy
Front seat air bags

DEBITS
Under powered

HOW THE RUNNERS-UP PLACED
FOLLOWING THE LINCOLN CONTINENTAL
2nd PLACE...1986 Mercedes-Benz 300E

Excellent handling and performance in a more sporting than luxury

Excellent handling and performance in a more sporting than luxury package. Does not have the quietness or interior space of the Continental. Also, to get below $20,000 in a Mercedes 300E you need to go back four more years.

3rd PLACE...1990 Cadillac Seville

Smooth V-8 power. A solid car greatly improved with the all-new 1992 model. Does not have the interior space of the Continental.

A CLOSER LOOK AT THE 1990 LINCOLN CONTINENTAL

SPECIFICATIONS:	Front engine, front-wheel drive, four-door luxury sedan.
ENGINE:	V-6
DISPLACEMENT:	3.8 liter
HORSEPOWER:	140 @ 3,8000 RPM
TORQUE:	225 foot-pounds @ 3,000 RPM
INDUCTION SYSTEM:	Electronic fuel injection
RECOMMENDED FUEL:	Unleaded regular
DRIVETRAIN:	Four-speed automatic
FRONT SUSPENSION:	Independent with computer-controlled air coil springs, anti-roll bar
REAR SUSPENSION:	Independent with computer-controlled air coil springs, anti-roll bar
STEERING TYPE:	Speed sensitive, variable-assist rack-and-pinion
TURNING CIRCLE (CURB-TO-CURB):	38.4 feet
BRAKE TYPE:	Front and rear disc with anti-lock power brakes
TIRE TYPE AND SIZE:	P205/70R15
WHEELBASE:	109.0 in.
LENGTH:	205.1 in.
WIDTH:	72.7 in.
HEIGHT:	55.6 in.
CURB WEIGHT:	3,623 pounds
TRUNK CARGO VOLUME:	19.1 cubic feet

ACCELERATION, 0-60 MPH: Approximately 10 seconds
FUEL CONSUMPTION: 17-24 miles per gallon

BEST LUXURY SEDAN
Price Range: Under $35,000

Prestige and status are equally important as performance, ride comfort, customer satisfaction and opulent surroundings when judging a luxury sedan in this price range.

THE CONTENDERS*	WHOLESALE	RETAIL
1990 Lexus LS 400	$27,550	$30,900
1988 Mercedes-Benz 420SEL . . .	$27,450	$30,800
1989 BMW 735i	$26,950	$30,275

*Prices of Contenders are base prices which may vary in range from those of the winning model.

The Winner

1990 LEXUS LS 400

It's no contest when selecting the best used luxury sedan under $35,000 — the clear winner is the 1990 Lexus LS 400. The Japanese luxury sedan, introduced in the 1990 model year, has been one of the biggest success stories in the auto industry.

Lexus, the premium division of Toyota, has stunned Mercedes-Benz, BMW and other luxury car manufacturers with its rare combination of ultra smoothness, quality build and value. Value is something not often found in the luxury car field. Many industry observers credit Lexus for driving Mercedes and BMW upmarket, where Lexus does not have a $70,000+

model.

While Mercedes and BMW had many years of a head start in reputation, status and prestige, the Lexus has been making up ground fast. During 1991, the LS 400 swept the quality awards given by the independent research firm of J.D. Power and Associates. In the Power "Initial Quality Study," a compilation of problems encountered by owners during the first 90 days of ownership, the LS 400 had the fewest problems ever recorded in the study's history. In the Power organization's "Customer Satisfaction Index," the LS 400 again finished No. 1.

The West Coast media introduction of the Lexus LS 400 in August 1989 was a preview of what was coming. The auto writers at Laguna Seca Raceway witnessed a very dramatic demonstration of smoothness and speed. An LS 400 — raised off the ground and balancing a pyramid of six filled wine glasses on its roof — was briskly accelerated to an indicated 156 mph.

There was relatively little noise, fuss or vibrations for the several minutes the four-door sedan held the high speed.

Richard L. Chitty, Lexus corporate manager for parts, service and customer relations, invited the journalists to step up to the "speeding" car and place a hand on the hood.

The speedometer indicated 156 mph, the tachometer needle was holding at 5,200 rpm, the rear tires were spinning at a blur, but little vibration could be detected from the car's hood or the still-balanced wine glasses.

While the demonstration car did not have to fight air or surface drag, the LS 400 is a legitimate 150-mph tourer.

"It's not the speed we run it at," said Chitty about the impressive demonstration. "What I really wanted to relate to was the smoothness and quietness. We were shifting gears – in a normal car you would have shaken off those glasses."

The high-speed static demonstration was just one of several staged by Lexus. The demonstrations pulled no punches in taking the competition head-on. The LS 400 was not compared with a hypothetical "Brand X," but in a side-by-side matchup with a Mercedes-Benz 420SEL and BMW 735i.

The hands-on comparisons by the media confirmed Lexus' claims that the LS 400 is quieter, smoother, more aerodynamic and had higher technology than its German counterparts.

The LS 400, with its original 1990 price of $35,000, also has a significant price advantage over the majority of its competition. For example, in the Mercedes fleet only the compact 190 series is priced less, with the 300E at $44,850, the 300SE at $51,400, the 420SEL at $61,210 and $72,280 for the 560SEL.

In innovation and technology, Mercedes closed the gap to Lexus with a complete redesign of its "S class" in 1992. However, prior models are a generation behind the Japanese luxury car.

Lexus claims the LS 400 has more than 300 world firsts in engineering and design including: a tilt-and-telescopic steering wheel combined with a driver's side airbag, the first traction control system in the U.S. market and the first automotive AM/FM stereo system by Nakamichi, with seven speakers, compact disc and cassette players.

A 1990 LS 400 is a good used car buy as the car is nearly identical to the 1991. The one major change in the '91 is a deeper-sounding horn. Ignoring that one difference could mean thousands of dollars in savings.

Size, Comfort and Style

The LS 400, which borrows many styling cues from Mercedes, fits in size between various Mercedes and BMW models. For example, the LS 400's wheelbase of 110.8 inches is closest to the Mercedes 300E at 110.2, but its overall length of 196.7 inches rivals the 202.6-inch length of the 300 SE.

Tipping the scales at 3,759 pounds, the LS 400 is heavier than the 300 models and is closer to the 3,885 pounds of the Mercedes 420SEL.

Under the hood and in acceleration, the Mercedes counterpart to the Lexus is the flagship 560SEL. The Lexus is powered by a 4.0-liter, four-camshaft

V-8 that generates 250 horsepower. The big Benz is pushed by a 5.6-liter V-8 rated at 238 horsepower. Both cars have top speeds of about 150 mph.

The LS 400 spoils its passengers with comfort. That is established when you first open the driver's door and note the steering wheel is pivoted up and out of the way to ease ingress and egress. The wheel automatically moves out of the way when the ignition key is removed.

Rear seat passengers are not short changed with the LS 400. There is good leg and knee room and headroom for six-foot tall passengers is not a problem.

Comfort also can be measured by the absolute silence of the V-8 engine. Without looking at the tachometer, it is nearly impossible to tell the LS 400 is running idle. The quietness continues at speed as the powerplant is complemented by the extremely low wind noise. The lack of wind noise is attributed to the LS 400's class-leading aerodynamic drag coefficient of 0.29.

Lexus has achieved near perfection with the LS 400's ride and handling. The car has both the firm control of a sports sedan and the forgiving ride of a luxury tourer. An optional electronic air suspension improves on the base suspension, if that is possible.

ENGINE AND DRIVETRAIN

The four-valve per cylinder Lexus LS 400 V-8 has been called one of the smoothest engines in the world. The all-aluminum powerplant also has aluminum valve lifters, a production first. The four-cam engine is rated at 250 horsepower at 5,600 rpm 260 foot-pounds of torque at 4,400 rpm.

Amazingly, the LS 400 engine is both powerful and economical. It is powerful enough to launch the nearly 3,800-pound sedan from 0-60 mph in 7.9 seconds and reach a top speed of 150 mph. At the same time, this jewel of an engine is EPA rated at 18 miles per gallon city and 23 in the highway mode. The fuel-efficient LS 400 escapes the federal "gas guzzler" tax. Meanwhile, seven of the twelve 1990 Mercedes models suffer the tax, which ranges from $500 on the 300TE station wagon to $1,500 on the 560SEL.

The wine glass performance would not be possible without the LS 400's advanced transmission. The four-speed electronically controlled transmission has selectable modes and is "intelligent." Via computer, the transmission communicates with the engine to retard ignition timing for a split second during shifts. The retarded timing reduces engine torque and allows for smoother shifts.

A console switch allows the driver to choose between "Normal" and "Power" shift programs. The "Power" mode shifts at higher engine speeds for better acceleration.

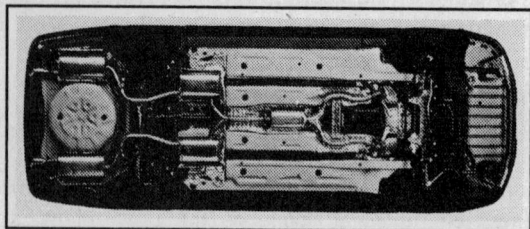

A traction control system is optional and greatly reduces wheel spin in slippery conditions. Working with the anti-lock braking system sensors, the unit detects wheel spin and automatically reduces power to the slipping tire by throttling down the engine and/or activating the rear brakes. A Lexus equipped with traction control, which can be switched off, will not spin the rear tires in gravel.

To eliminate driveshaft vibration, Lexus engineers aligned the engine crankshaft and two-piece driveshaft in a straight line.

HANDLING

The LS 400 has handling capabilities that rival the best European sports sedans. The LS 400 uses an independent double-wishbone suspension anchored off an extremely rigid body structure. The front upper wishbone is mounted high on the chassis to optimize caster and camber geometry at speed.

The rear suspension has multi-links that are designed to increase toe-in during hard cornering for improved stability. Gas-filled shock absorbers help maximize stability and front- and rear-stabilizer bars minimize body lean during cornering.

An optional air-suspension system automatically adjusts vehicle height, spring rate and dampening force for an even more comfortable ride. The air suspension also has a dual modes — "Normal" or "Sport" — for cruising or spirited driving, respectively.

Brakes

The LS 400's world-class brakes are 10.83-inch diameter ventilated front discs, matched with 11.46-inch vented rear discs. An anti-lock braking system with four sensors is standard. The ABS prevents tire lockup and gives steering control under panic stops or slippery conditions.

Where the rubber meets the road, the LS 400 has P205/65R15 Goodyear Eagle GA high-performance radials that were designed exclusively for the LS 400. A no-charge option are all-weather Dunlop D80 V4 radials. Either tires are mounted on 6-inch wide, 15-inch alloy wheels. Stopping distance from 60 mph is 135 feet.

Ride Quality

Ride quality is literally unmatched. The LS 400 can equal any domestic luxury liner for comfort and quiet ride. Wind noise is practically nonexistent and the engine does its work silently. Shifts from the "intelligent" automatic transmission can hardly be felt.

The multi-link rear independent suspension allows the LS 400 to keep in balance and form even when cornering over rutted roads. The Goodyear Eagle GA high-performance radials were designed exclusively for the LS 400 to provide a good ride and high-performance.

The optional air-suspension system, automatically adjusts vehicle height, spring rate and dampening force, offering an even more comfortable ride.

INTERIOR

The interior of the LS 400 is very inviting, right from the swing away steering wheel that eases entry and exit. Cloth upholstery is standard with a leather package optional. The front buckets give good support and have a host of power adjustments. The following adjustments are all power operated: front to back track adjustment, seatback recline, driver's seat height adjustment, seat rake angle and lumbar support.

The tilting and telescoping steering wheel is an industry first to include an airbag. In addition to the swing away feature of the steering wheel, an optional feature will automatically set for two different drivers from a programmed memory the position of the outside mirrors, the height of the headrest and the position of the upper shoulder belt mount. The four-spoke leather-wrapped steering wheel frames

the brightly lit instrument panel, which is dominated by a large speedometer and tachometer.

Nearly every power and accessory feature is standard. One of the few options, a hands-free cellular telephone, automatically lowers the volume of the stereo when the phone is in use.

The rear seat can acommodate three average-sized adults comfortably and has good leg and headroom. A pair of six-footers can sit at the rear outboard positions.

SUMMARY

Toyota did the near impossible and hit a home run its first time at bat in the luxury car division. The Lexus LS 400 is the new standard of fit-and-finish and value in the luxury car market.

Lexus came out of no where to displace Mercedes and Acura from the top spot in the J.D. Power and Associates "Customer Satisfaction Index."

Just in its third model year, used LS 400 models are scarce and available cars are going for premium prices. The resale value of the LS 400 is the highest of any luxury car.

1990 LEXUS LS 400

ASSETS	DEBITS
High customer satisfaction	Limited availability
Extremely smooth V-8 engine	
Excellent ride and handling	

HOW THE RUNNERS-UP PLACED
FOLLOWING THE LEXUS 400

2nd PLACE...The 1988 Mercedes-Benz 420SEL

A close physical match to the LS 400, but can not equal the performance and value. Mercedes closed the performance gap with its all-new '92 models, but the price gap grows.

3rd PLACE...The 1989 BMW 735i

Even the very smooth inline six of the 735i is not a match for the LS 400 V-8 engine.

A CLOSER LOOK AT THE 1990 LEXUS LS 400

SPECIFICATIONS: Front engine, rear-wheel drive, four-door luxury sedan. Options include leather package, air suspension and traction control.

ENGINE: V-8

DISPLACEMENT: 4.0 liter

HORSEPOWER: 250 @ 5,600 RPM

TORQUE: 260 foot-pounds @ 4,400 RPM

INDUCTION SYSTEM: Multi-port fuel injection

RECOMMENDED FUEL: Unleaded premium

DRIVETRAIN: Four-speed automatic

FRONT SUSPENSION: Independent, double wishbone with coil springs

REAR SUSPENSION: Independent, double wishbone with coil springs

STEERING TYPE: Speed-sensing power rack-and-pinion

TURNING CIRCLE (CURB-TO-CURB): 36.1 feet

BRAKE TYPE: Power-assisted front and rear disc with anti-lock braking system

TIRE TYPE AND SIZE: P205/65R15

WHEELBASE: 110.8 in.

LENGTH: 196.7 in.

WIDTH: 71.7 in.

HEIGHT: 55.3 in.

CURB WEIGHT: 3,759 pounds

TRUNK CARGO VOLUME: 14.4-cubic feet

ACCELERATION, 0-60 MPH: 7.9 seconds

FUEL CONSUMPTION: 18-23 miles per gallon

BEST ULTRA-LUXURY SEDAN
Price Range: Over $35,000

An ultra-luxury sedan is bigger than life and has ultra performance, ultra comfort, ultra amenities, ultra quality , ultra safety , ultra status, ultra technology and costs ultra dollars. With ultra-luxury sedans, cost is no object.

THE CONTENDERS*	WHOLESALE	RETAIL
1991 BMW 750iL	$55,000	$56,700
1991 Jaguar XJ6 Vanden Plas . . .	$32,600	$36,250
1991 Mercedes-Benz 560SEL . . .	$54,100	$59,200

*Prices of Contenders are base prices which may vary in range from those of the winning model.

The Winner

1991 MERCEDES-BENZ 560SEL

If you are in the market for a used ultra-luxury car, expect to pay some serious dollars. But also expect to receive the finest craftsmanship, the highest standard of fit and finish, the ultimate in safety, reliability and dealer service, a smooth and powerful engine, a huge rear seating area, and the envy of all your neighbors.

Ultra-luxury cars are expensive and no matter how you figure it, they are not cost effective. It is very hard to justify an automobile that costs more than the median price of a house. They use a lot of gasoline, are expensive to maintain and expensive to insure.

But if you can afford an ultra-luxury car — even a used one — don't sweat the small stuff.

The best ultra-luxury car over $30,000 — about double that — is the 1991 Mercedes-Benz 560SEL.

A used '91 560SEL, with its current wholesale value of $54,100 and an average retail of $59,200, is actually quite a bargain. New, the 560SEL had a suggested retail price of $75,100, plus the buyer has to pay a federal gas guzzler tax of $1,300. If this is not bad enough, there is also a ten percent luxury tax for any amount more than $30,000. And don't forget adding sales taxes.

With all the taxes, a new '91 560SEL rolled out the door over $84,000. Meanwhile, the used car buyer — excluded from the gas guzzler and luxury tax — is hit for just $65,710, a savings of $20,081!

The savings are even greater when you compare a used '91 with its '92 counterpart. The new generation of S Class Mercedes debuted in '92 and the new top-of-the-line 12-cylinder 600SEL has a suggested retail price of $128,000, plus the various taxes.

The 560SEL is the flagship of the S Class of Mercedes-Benz sedans that includes the 300SE, 300SEL and 420 SEL.

The "L" in the designation signifies a long-wheelbase model. The 5.5 inch longer wheelbase of the "L" version equates into much greater rear seat room.

The 560SEL has a 121.1-inch wheelbase and an overall length of 208.1 inches. Rear seat headroom and leg room is within about an inch of the front seat accommodations.

The 560SEL is powered by a 5.6-liter V-8 rated at 238 horsepower and is capable of moving 4,100 pounds from a standing start to 60 mph in 7.4 seconds.

The list of standard features on the 560SEL is very long and includes: cruise control, hydropneumatic level control for the rear axle, alloy wheels, limited-slip differential, four-wheel disc brakes with anti-lock braking system, power-assisted steering, four-wheel automatic transmission, electrically heated windshield washer system, halogen fog lights, headlamp wipers and washers, electrically adjusted and heated outside mirrors, AM/FM stereo with cassette, automatic climate control, first aid kit, electrically telescoping steering column, no-cost choice of leather or velour upholstery, power windows, electric sliding sunroof with rear pop-up feature, driver's side and front passenger airbags and electrically heated and adjustable front seats with head restraints.

The short list of options includes an electrically operated rear window shade, front seats with electro-pneumatically adjustable, orthopedic backrests and a four-place seating package.

The 560SEL also comes standard with that special class and status exclusive to only the German automaker. Just one time behind the wheel of a 560SEL will spoil you forever. Anything you drive from then on will not likely match up.

The car has a solid feel, as if it was machined from one solid billet of steel. The performance is surprising considering its size, and the comfort and ride are second to none.

Just ask Britain's Princess Diana. Princess Di recently created a stir with union leaders and her subjects when she sold her Jaguar XJS to lease a Mercedes-Benz S Class. A Buckingham Palace spokeswoman said Diana leased the Mercedes for her personal use, but would continue to attend public engagements in her official Jaguar XJ6.

Size, Comfort and Style

The Mercedes 560SEL is big on size, comfort and style. The 4,100-pound sedan stands on a 121.1-inch wheelbase and has an overall length of 208.1 inches. It definitely is a big car, but its outstanding road feel and responsiveness make you forget its size.

The comfort level of the Mercedes is excellent with the 5.5 inch additional wheelbase of the 560SEL. All the extra inches can be found in the back seat area. Rear leg and headroom is limousine standard and within one inch of the generous front passenger section.

The long wheelbase and Teutonic suspension tuning give the 560SEL a comfortable and well-controlled ride. For long trips it cannot be beat as it effortlessly rolls up the miles. Hydro-pneumatic shock absorbers and automatic level control keep the car at an even keel no matter the load.

The subtle aerodynamic theme of the 560SEL was introduced in 1980 and further refined with the latest '92 model. The new body style has reduced the drag coefficient from a very good 0.37 to an amazing 0.31. However, the '92 keeps many of the styling cues of the previous model. The wide and stable stance, flush headlamps, strong B-pillar, horizontal slatted MB grille and of course the stand-up three-pointed star. There is no mistaking the family resemblance and the 560SEL's stature and class level.

ENGINE AND DRIVETRAIN

The 560SEL is propelled by a silent and smooth 5.6-liter V-8 that produces 238 horsepower at 4,800 rpm and 287 foot-pounds of torque at 3,500 rpm. The all-aluminum engine has a single overhead camshaft for the each V-8 bank and uses Bosch KE III Electro-mechanical fuel injection. Unleaded premium gasoline is required.

The potent engine pushes the 4,100-pound sedan from 0-60 miles per hour in just 7.4 seconds. The top speed is electronically limited to 155 miles per hour. This performance comes at the expensive of fuel economy, the 560SEL is EPA rated at 14 miles per gallon city and 17 mpg highway.

The 560SEL has a smooth-shifting four-speed automatic transmission. This transmission can be shifted manually, holding that specific gear indefinitely until the shift lever is again moved. The final drive ratio is 2.47:1, which allows the 560SEL to effortlessly cruise at 60 mph at just 2,050 rpm.

A new option in '91 ensured that all the 238 horsepower did not end up in tire smoke. The ASR automatic slip control uses wheel-speed sensors to detect wheel slip, using two different methods to bring it under control. The first is by applying the brakes to the drive wheel or wheels about to spin. The second is via an "electronic accelerator pedal" that reduces engine output to match the available traction. Both actions occur without input from the driver, in fact the driver can floor the gas pedal and the engine will not race if the tires are spinning with ASR.

In addition to providing improved traction, ASR aids in maintaining directional stability in turns, during lane changes or in evasive maneuvers. A dashboard indicator light — which illuminates whenever ASR is activated — is an important part of the system, informing the driver of the road conditions and vehicle dynamics, so speed and driving technique can be adjusted accordingly in slippery conditions.

HANDLING

Big Mercedes sedans are famous for their surprising ability to go around a corner at speed. British driving champion Stirling Moss once took a carload of auto journalists around a race track in near record time driving a huge Mercedes 600 Pullman.

Mercedes handling is engineered for Europe's no-speed limit autobahns. If a Mercedes is stable and well controlled at 130 mph, America's 55 miles per hour speed limits will not tax the suspension.

The front independent suspension consists of double A-arms, coil springs, anti-roll bar and gas-pressurized shock absorbers. The suspension geometry includes anti-dive action and zero-offset steering that maintains straight ahead control during adverse conditions such as a flat tire.

The rear independent suspension has semi-trailing arms, coil springs, anti-roll bar, hydro-pneumatic units that act as shock absorbers, automatic level control and limited-slip differential.

The steering system is a recirculating ball type with power assist and a steering damper. The 560SEL's steering has an excellent on-center feel, which makes for responsive feedback and steering control. The four contact patches are P205/65VR15 high-performance radial tires.

Brakes

Power front and rear disc brakes are standard. The front ventilated discs measure 11.8 inches. The rear solid discs are 11.0 inches. A standard anti-lock braking system prevents tire lockup and maintains steering control during severe braking and slippery conditions. From 60 miles per hour, the 560SEL stops in 152 feet.

Ride Quality

Ride quality is excellent with the long 121.1-inch wheelbase and solid vault-like body construction dampening bumps and rough surfaces. The sophisticated rear suspension is extremely well mannered and can handle bumpy corners with excellent control.

The ride quality is at its best when cruising effortlessly and silently on the freeway. The cruise control is set, the stereo is filling the interior with music and the miles and scenery just keep passing by.

INTERIOR

The stretched wheelbase of the 560SEL gives limousine-like room to stretch from either the front or back seats. The 560SEL for no extra charge was available with either leather or velour interior.

The front bucket seats and headrests are electrically adjustable. Electrically heated front seats are standard, with optional electro-pneumatically adjustable orthopedic backrests. The rear seat passengers also have headrests, standard electrically adjustable recline and heated seating areas.

A rare interior option is the four-place seating package. This option places four individual, electric bucket seats in the 560SEL. The rear buckets are separated by a rear storage console.

The instrument panel of the 560SEL is complete with large speedometer and tachometer and a complement of gauges that include oil pressure, coolant temperature, fuel economy indicator, outside temperature and quartz chronometer. In addition, there are warning indicators for exterior lamp failure, front brake pad wear, low engine oil, and engine and windshield washer fluid levels.

The interior also boasts a pair of front seat airbags, protective knee bolsters and emergency tensioning retractors for the three-point inertial reel seat belts that enhance their effectiveness. The front shoulder belts adjust to suit the height of the driver or passenger.

SUMMARY

The 1991 Mercedes-Benz 560SEL is the best ultra-luxury sedan because of its leading world-class performance, ride, comfort and reputation. The 560SEL is a very powerful car that is at home on the high-speed autobahn or cruising silently at 60 miles per hour.

With the federal gas guzzler and luxury car taxes on new vehicles, the used 560SEL is even a bit of a bargain. The '91 560SEL has the same basic look, status and class of the latest '92 S Class, but costs tens of thousands of dollars less.

1991 MERCEDES-BENZ 560SEL

ASSETS
Powerful V-8
Anti-lock braking system
Driver's side airbag
Ultimate in status

DEBITS
Expensive
High fuel consumption

HOW THE RUNNERS-UP PLACED
FOLLOWING THE MERCEDES-BENZ 560SEL
2nd PLACE... 1991 BMW 750iL
Powerful and smooth V-12. The 560SEL has more interior room, better resale value and more status.
3rd PLACE... 1991 Jaguar XJ6 Vanden Plas
Vanden Plas has opulent interior treatment. The smooth six-cylinder engine is no match in power or smoothness to its V-8 and V-12 rivals.

A CLOSER LOOK AT THE 1991 MERCEDES-BENZ 560SEL

SPECIFICATIONS: Front engine, rear-wheel drive, four-door luxury sedan.
ENGINE: V-8
DISPLACEMENT: 5.6 liter
HORSEPOWER: 238 @ 4,800 RPM
TORQUE: 287 foot-pounds @ 3,500 RPM
INDUCTION SYSTEM: Electro-mechanical fuel injection

RECOMMENDED FUEL:	Unleaded premium
DRIVETRAIN:	Four-speed automatic
FRONT SUSPENSION:	Independent double control arm with coil springs, gas-pressurized shock absorbers, anti-roll bar
REAR SUSPENSION:	Independent semi-trailing arm with coil springs, gas-pressurized shock absorbers, anti-roll bar
STEERING TYPE:	Power assisted recirculating ball-type
TURNING CIRCLE (CURB-TO-CURB):	40.6 feet
BRAKE TYPE:	Power-assisted front and rear discs with anti-locking system
TIRE TYPE AND SIZE:	P205/65R15
WHEELBASE:	121.1 in.
LENGTH:	208.1 in.
WIDTH:	71.7 in.
HEIGHT:	56.3 in.
CURB WEIGHT:	4,100 pounds
TRUNK CARGO VOLUME:	15.2-cubic feet
ACCELERATION, 0-60 MPH:	7.4 seconds
FUEL CONSUMPTION:	14-17 miles per gallon

BEST SPORTS COUPE
Price Range: Under $10,000

The goal here is sports car handling, style and excitement with the usefulness of a rear seat. Sporty, but practicality, is the key.

THE CONTENDERS*	WHOLESALE	RETAIL
1990 Ford Probe GL	$7,125	$8,275
1990 Plymouth Laser RS	$7,925	$9,100
1987 Toyota Supra Turbo	$7,850	$9,125

*Prices of Contenders are base prices which may vary in range from those of the winning model.

The Winner

1987 TOYOTA SUPRA TURBO

When you want a sports car, but must settle for something a bit more practical, a sports coupe is what you want.

If you want the best used sports coupe for less than $10,000, you definitely want a 1987 Toyota Supra Turbo. With the Supra Turbo there is no settling for less. The flagship Toyota has it all — power, smoothness, handling, luxury and style. And at less than $10,000 it is a tremendous bargain. A bargain that compares very favorably with the hottest new sports coupe — the 1992 Lexus SC 300. If you lust after a new Lexus SC 300 sports coupe, be prepared to write a check for at least $31,100. However, further investigation shows the Supra Turbo and SC 300 — both manufactured by Toyota — share much in common with each other.

Both are powered by 3.0-liter, inline sixes with double-overhead camshafts and 24 valves. The normally aspirated Lexus is rated at 225 horsepower and the turbocharged Supra at 230 horses. The Supra engine is just shy of the 250 horsepower, 4.0-liter V-8 found in the Lexus SC 400. The SC 400, which lists for approximately $40,000, is only available with an automatic. The SC 300, like the Supra, is available with either a five-speed manual or four-speed automatic transmission.

Both the SC 300 and Supra have four-wheel, double wishbone suspension and four-wheel disc brakes. The SC 300 is 9.2 inches longer in overall length and the Supra weighs 36 pounds more at 3,530.

The Supra can also match its higher-priced Lexus cousins in standard amenities point-for-point. The Supra comes standard with AM/FM cassette, automatic temperature control, electric windows, central locking, electric adjustable outside mirrors, and cruise control. Options include an all-electric controls package that includes power seat adjusters — recline, height, lumbar and back-and-forth tracking — for the driver's seat, and a removable roof panel.

Both the SC 300 and Supra Turbo offer an almost ideal combination of luxury and performance. They both are smooth, fast and refined. For the sport coupe bargain hunter, a used '87 Supra Turbo is less than one-third the price of a new Lexus SC 300 and less than one-fourth the price of a SC 400.

The Supra started out as the top-of-the-line Celica and shared platforms with the sporty Toyota. Supra became its own distinctive model in 1982. By splitting off the two cars, Toyota now had the Celica in the entry-level sports coupe market and the upscale Supra in the luxury performance segment.

The '82 Supra shared many common body components from the windshield on back. The Supra had a four-inch longer wheelbase and an inline six-cylinder engine. The Supra also differed from the Celica with a independent rear suspension and upgraded interior and equipment level.

For 1986 the Supra received a facelift that softened the car's overall lines and gave the car a more rounded aerodynamic look.

In the powerplant area, it has nearly been a Supra tradition to slightly increase the big six's horsepower each year. The biggest jump ever occurred in 1987 — our pick — when the Supra debuted a turbocharged engine worth 230 horsepower.

The exhaust-driven supercharger is exactly what puts the Supra on top of the sports coupe market. The 3.0-liter six gives the 3,530-pound hatchback good low-end performance. The mild boost from the turbo continues the momentum throughout the mid-range and the top-end to the Supra's 140 mph top speed. On the way to nearly three times the national speed limit, the Supra sprints from 0-60 mph in 6.7 seconds.

The Supra also has something very important in any used car, a long history and tradition of reliability and durability. Toyota products have long been at the top of the charts in surveys conducted by J.D. Power and Associates for fewest problems and for customer satisfaction.

Size, Comfort and Style

The Supra is no lightweight. Packed on its 102.2-inch wheelbase and 181.9-inch overall length is 3,530 pounds. Every pound is accounted for and can be felt in its solid road feel. This is definitely not a tinny car, but a hefty automobile built for durability and longevity — two traits that are very much sought after when selecting a used car.

Front seat passengers have a lot of room in all directions — shoulder, leg and head. In the back seat of the 2+2 coupe however, it's strictly for children or short trips for adults. A better idea is to fold the rear seatbacks forward and use the area for an additional luggage space. The Supra's 12.8-cubic feet of trunk space jumps to 20.6-cubic feet when the seatbacks are tumbled forward.

The Supra can match standard features with almost any luxury car. The long list includes AM/FM cassette, automatic temperature control, electric windows, central locking, electric adjustable outside mirrors, and cruise control. If you need even more creature comforts, include an all-electric controls package that includes power seat adjusters — recline, height, lumbar and back-and-forth tracking — for the driver's seat, and a removable roof panel. The removable sport roof is larger than a sunroof and really gives the Supra a convertible look and feel.

While the Supra's exterior received a makeover in '86 that smoothed out the lines and gave it an "aero" influence, the basic proportions remain classic pony car — a long hood and short rear deck.

The heft of the Supra can be seen in the width, substantial stance and 58.5-inch front and rear track of the car. Adding to the wide-track look are the wide 16-inch by 7-inch alloy wheels shod with low-profile P225/50VR-16 Goodyear Eagle VR50 high-performance radial tires.

ENGINE AND DRIVETRAIN

The base inline six engine on the Supra displaces 3.0 liters and is rated at 200 horsepower at 6,000 rpm and 188 foot-pounds of torque at 3,600 rpm. The powerplant features double overhead camshafts that manipulate four-valves per cylinder. The big six evolved from the original Supra six that displaced 2.8 liters and produced 165 horsepower.

The Supra six received a turbocharger in 1987 that boosted the horsepower to 230. For a turbocharger installation, the horsepower gain of 15 percent was very minimal. For example, when a turbocharger is added to the Mitsubishi Eclipse, horsepower jumps from 135 to 195 — a 44 percent gain.

However, Toyota engineers were not looking for ultimate horsepower, but a wider powerband and improved low-end torque. In the torque department, the figures climbed 31 percent, from 188 foot-pounds to 246 foot-pounds. Just as important, the higher torque level of the turbocharged engine is achieved at 400 rpms lower than the peak torque of the normally aspirated engine.

The improvement in torque can really be felt in everyday driving situations. The car is easy to launch from a stop and the throttle response and acceleration at low- to mid-speeds is instantaneous. With the Supra Turbo there is no turbo lag, that condition where engine response is weak until the exhaust gases and rpm increase enough to spin the turbo and build boost. With the Supra Turbo, the generous low-end torque launches the car smartly — 0-60 in 6.7 seconds — and then the turbocharger takes over for the charge up to the 6,500 rpm redline.

The mild boost also ensures that the engine life of the Turbo should match the life of the normally aspirated version.

The willing engine deals out smooth and progressive power. It does not "get on the cam" or throw you suddenly back into the seat like some "on-or-off" turbo cars. The power is linear and very flexible. The Supra Turbo is as close to the feel of a healthy V-8 as any six can be.

Either engine is available with a slick-shifting five-speed manual transmission or a four-speed automatic with overdrive. The automatic is a good match with the Turbo. The extra power of the Turbo makes up for any power loss from the automatic and the torque multiplication and smooth application of power from the automatic makes the Supra even more turbine-like in smoothness.

The automatic has a final drive ratio of 4.3:1. On the manual units, the final drive is 4.30:1 for the standard Supra and 3.72:1 for the Turbo.

HANDLING

The Supra does not let you forget it is a substantial car in weight. However, the car's 3,530 pounds are well balanced with 52 percent positioned over the front tires and 48 percent over the rear.

The weight also can be felt in fast cornering maneuvers, where the Supra will lean into the corner, take a set, and hold its line. The handling is very stable and very easy to control and position.

The Supra's handling prowess comes from its very sophisticated suspension that features four-wheel independent suspension with double wishbone A-arms at each corner, coil springs and front and rear anti-roll bars. Another option is Toyota's electronically modulated suspension which automatically adjusts shock absorber firmness to match driving conditions.

Brakes

With a top speed of 140 mph and 3,530 pounds to stop, the Supra Turbo better have good brakes and it definitely does. The power-assisted, four-wheel disc brakes include massive 11.9-inch vented front rotors and

11.5-inch rear disc brakes. The stopping action also benefits from the good weight distribution, wishbone suspension and wide 50-series radial tires. From 60 miles per hour, the Supra Turbo stops in 146 feet. Overall braking operation is rated excellent.

Ride Quality

While the Supra has many luxury car features, its ride is more like a sports car. However, the substantial weight of the car translates behind the wheel to a very solid and secure ride. The very rigid unibody structure also contributes to the solid feel of quality construction.

The optional electronically modulated suspension which automatically adjusts shock absorber firmness to match driving conditions also has a two mode manual setting — normal and sport. The normal setting improves the ride quality slightly, only because the sport setting is not overly firm and also gives good ride comfort.

INTERIOR

The Supra's luxury car leanings can be seen in the plush interior. The front seats are adjustable to fit any size individual and with the optional all-electric controls package the power driver's seat adjusts seat recline, height, lumbar and back-and-forth tracking. Cloth upholstery is standard with leather optional.

The interior is roomy for the front passengers, with the rear 2+2 seats a tight fit and best for children or short trips for adults. The rear seatbacks tumble forward to increase the luggage capacity by 7.8-cubic feet.

The stick shift falls at hand from the center console and the instrument panel is clear and easy to read.

Standard creature comforts include AM/FM cassette, automatic temperature control, electric windows, central locking, electric adjustable outside mirrors, and cruise control. The sound system has six speakers and a premium sound system is optional.

SUMMARY

The 1987 Toyota Supra Turbo is a great buy at less than $10,000 in the used sports coupe market. It has the power, handling and luxury of new sports coupes costing four times as much. The '87 is the first year the Turbo became available and is the model to purchase. The addition of a turbocharger further enhances the smooth and progressive power that has been a Supra trademark.

In this price range, the competition cannot match the Supra Turbo's power, smoothness and luxury. In addition there is also the Toyota reputation for quality and reliability. All in all, a hard combination to beat.

1987 TOYOTA SUPRA TURBO

ASSETS
Powerful turbo engine
Luxury car amenities
Toyota reputation

DEBITS
Requires premium fuel
16-inch tires expensive to replace

HOW THE RUNNERS-UP PLACED
FOLLOWING THE TOYOTA SUPRA TURBO
2nd PLACE...1990 Ford Probe GL
The Probe outsells its Mazda MX-6 twin and is available with a V-6. Both cars are built in Flat Rock, Mich. by Mazda. Lacks the luxury of the Supra.
3rd PLACE...1990 Plymouth Laser
A very nice package, strictly a 2+2. The Laser and Eagle Talon and Mitsubishi Eclipse clones are assembled by Diamond Star at Normal, Ill. Does not have the power and luxury features of the Supra.

A CLOSER LOOK AT THE 1987 TOYOTA SUPRA TURBO

SPECIFICATIONS:	Front engine, rear-wheel drive, two-door coupe.
ENGINE:	Inline six
DISPLACEMENT:	5.7 liter
HORSEPOWER:	230 @ 5,600 RPM
TORQUE:	246 foot-pounds @ 3,200 RPM
INDUCTION SYSTEM:	Electronic fuel injection with turbocharger
RECOMMENDED FUEL:	Unleaded premium
DRIVETRAIN:	Five-speed manual

FRONT SUSPENSION: Independent double wishbone, gas-pressurized shock absorbers, coil springs

REAR SUSPENSION: Independent double wishbone, gas-pressurized shock absorbers, coil springs

STEERING TYPE: Power-assisted rack-and-pinion

TURNING CIRCLE (CURB-TO-CURB): 35.4 feet

BRAKE TYPE: Power-assisted front disc/rear disc

TIRE TYPE AND SIZE: P225/50VR16

WHEELBASE: 102.2 in.

LENGTH: 181.9 in.

WIDTH: 68.7 in.

HEIGHT: 51.6 in.

CURB WEIGHT: 3,530 pounds

TRUNK CARGO VOLUME: 12.8-cubic feet, 20.6-cubic feet with rear seat folded down

ACCELERATION, 0-60 MPH: 6.7 seconds

FUEL CONSUMPTION: 17-22 miles per gallon

BEST SPORTS COUPE
Price Range: Under $20,000

The goal here is sports car handling, style and excitement with the practicality of a rear seat. Upping the ante to $20,000 adds the extra parameter of status and luxury amenities.

THE CONTENDERS*

	WHOLESALE	RETAIL
1989 Acura Legend Coupe	$14,975	$17,575
1991 Honda Prelude Si	$12,800	$15,125
1991 Volkswagen Corrado	$13,075	$15,400

*Prices of Contenders are base prices which may vary in range from those of the winning model.

The Winner

1989 ACURA LEGEND COUPE

Twenty thousand dollars is a lot of money and it can also buy a lot of used sports coupe. In this league, that means a world-class automobile that does everything well - stops, accelerates, handles, is fuel efficient and is a comfortable touring car.

Upping the ante to $20,000 also adds the extra parameter of status and luxury amenities. The sports coupes in this price range are somewhat unique and not as common as the garden variety of Nissan 240SX, Toyota Celica or Ford Probe.

The best used sports coupe under $20,000 is the Acura Legend Coupe. The

Legend Coupe tops the runners-up with its refinement, powerful and smooth V-6 and high-quality build. The Acura line has also been at the top or near the top of the J.D. Power and Associates surveys for quality and customer satisfaction.

The '89 Legend Coupe is an excellent used car buy, fitting comfortably beneath our $20,000 maximum. Because the demand for used Legend Sedans is strong, the Sedan returns more of its original value in resale than the Coupe, which costs several thousand dollars more when both are new. This unusual depreciation turnabout makes the Coupe an even better used car buy.

The replacement cost for a brand new coupe took a quantum leap with the 1991 debut of an all-new Legend Coupe that is larger and more powerful. The latest Coupe retails for more than $30,000, with the top-of-the-line LS Coupe topping $36,000.

The Acura marque was introduced by Honda in 1986 as a new "premium" line of luxury cars sold separately from Honda dealerships. The new brand's first car was the Legend Sedan and the four-cylinder Integra sports sedan. The following year the Legend Coupe was introduced.

Acura automobiles have been winners on the sales floor, in award competitions, in consumer satisfaction and at the race track. In sales, Acura sold 52,869 units for the '86 calendar year. The following year, Acura's first full sales year, sales reached 109,470 — outdistancing Volvo, 106,539; Mercedes-Benz, 90,832; and BMW, 89,487.

The strong sales have been boosted by the numerous awards Acura cars have received including: "Ten Best Cars," *Car and Driver* magazine for the Legend Sedan and Coupe; and "1987 Import Car of the Year," *Motor Trend* magazine, all for the Legend Coupe. Acura also took top honors in the J.D. Power and Associates "Consumer Satisfaction" survey in 1987, 1988, 1989 and 1990; Mercedes-Benz was second. On the racing circuit, the Integra has dominated the IMSA International Sedan series, winning titles in 1986-88.

The remarkable success of Acura spawned other Japanese automakers to introduce their own luxury premium lines: Nissan launched Infiniti, Toyota created Lexus. Mazda has also announced plans for its own upscale brand.

The Legend Coupe has a shorter 106.5-inch wheelbase than the Sedan it is based on. Overall length is down 1.4 inches to 188.0-inches for the Coupe. The Coupe uses a larger 2.7-liter version of the Sedan's 2.5-liter V-6 and has a 160 to 151 horsepower advantage. The two cars also share the same front suspension and front end styling. However, the Coupe has its own unique design from the firewall back.

Overall, the Coupe exterior, with its thin roof pillars and large glass area, has more of a wedge shape than the Sedan and is more aerodynamic. According to Acura figures, the Coupe's coefficient of drag is 0.30, compared to 0.32 for the Sedan.

The Coupe lineup is made up of three models: the standard Coupe, L and top-line LS. The L and LS have higher trim levels and more standard features. The L and LS models include electrically adjustable seats, heated outside mirrors, anti-lock brakes, a security system and an information center that includes a trip computer and a maintenance monitoring system. The LS has a premium Bose sound system, passive automatic seat belts for front passengers and a driver's airbag. Add about $1,200 for the 1989 L and $2,100 for the '89 LS.

All the Coupe models have the excellent quality, fit and finish Acura has built its reputation and short heritage on. The Coupe is most often compared to the BMW 6-Series sport coupe — but the 1989 6-Series retails at about $30,000.

Size, Comfort and Style

When Acura created the Coupe from the Sedan, it maintained a great majority of the Sedan's comfort by only slightly downsizing the Coupe. The Coupe's wheelbase and overall length is within two inches of the Sedan. The "smaller" Coupe, at a curb weight of 3,220 pounds, is actually heavier than the Sedan by 65 pounds.

By making such small sacrifices in size, Acura was able to match the solid road feel and interior comfort of the Sedan with the more sporting coupe. Overall, the ride is firm and well controlled.

Unlike most coupes on the market, the Legend Coupe not only has comfortable accommodations for front seat passengers, but also has a surprisingly roomy, rear seat area. Not just children, large dogs and packages can find comfort here, but actual full-sized adults.

The styling of the Coupe picks up on the cues from the BMW 6-series sports coupe. The BMW influence can be seen in the Coupe's proportions, four-place seating and particularly the thin roof pillars and large expanses of glass. The large greenhouse also has the added benefit of excellent visibility — 323 degrees — for the driver.

The clean exterior with its very low coefficient of drag also enhances the driving comfort of the Coupe by reducing wind noise at high speed. The slick exterior includes a pronounced wedge shape, flush headlights and door handles, mild front air dam and rear spoiler, and a flowing back window and rear deck.

ENGINE AND DRIVETRAIN

When Acura was planning the Coupe, it wanted to improve the low-speed performance of the Sedan's 2.5-liter V-6. It achieved this by enlarging the bore 3 mm, resulting in a larger, 2.7-liter unit.

The four-valves-per-cylinder aluminum block engine then received Honda's Variable Intake Control System. This two-stage system is basically two manifolds in one. At low speeds, the intake charge is directed to a relatively small intake tube to generate high intake air velocity for good low-speed performance. As the rpm increase to 3,200 rpm, a second intake tube begins to open up and feed the engine more air. Honda first used this two-stage concept with its high-performance motorcycles.

With Honda's programmed fuel injection and other mechanical tricks, the 2.7-liter V-6 develops 160 horsepower at 5,900 rpm and 162 foot-pounds of torque at 4,500 rpm. This compares favorably with the Sedan which is rated at 151 horsepower and 154 foot-pounds of torque.

The gain of just 8 foot-pounds of torque does not seem significant, but the difference is clearly felt behind the wheel and with the stopwatch. The Coupe will sprint from 0-60 miles per hour in 7.7 seconds — 0.4 seconds quicker than the slightly lighter Sedan. The Coupe has a top speed of 130 miles per hour, the Sedan 129. The coupe is EPA rated at 18 miles per gallon city and 22 mpg on the highway. Many Coupe owners report actual mileage is higher and 25 mpg is not uncommon on the highway.

The front-wheel-drive Coupe comes standard with a smooth shifting five-speed manual transmission. The one complaint about the Coupe's powertrain is a somewhat vague clutch that can be too light and difficult to feel when it engages.

A four-speed automatic transmission is optional. The two-mode automatic allows the driver to choose a "Sport" setting that raises shift points and torque converter lock-up for more performance. The automatic, unlike in most cars, does not steal much power and performance from the engine.

Overall, the Coupe's engine and drivetrain are very strong and has Honda's well-earned reputation for reliability, durability and low-maintenance.

HANDLING

The greatest praise for a front-wheel-drive car is that it handles and drives like a rear-wheel-drive car. The Coupe does not have the heavy understeer and torque steer found in lesser front-wheel-drive vehicles. That is only possible with a sophisticated suspension system and a well-balanced chassis.

The Legend Coupe's independent front suspension consists of a double wishbone A-arms with coil springs, gas-pressurized shocks and an anti-roll bar. The anti-roll bar uses ball-ends instead of the more conventional bushings for better action.

The Coupe's independent rear suspension also uses double wishbones with coil springs, gas-pressurized shocks and an anti-roll bar. Most front-wheel-drive automobiles, including the excellent handling Volkswagen Corrado, use a similar, less expensive torsion beam rear suspension.

The Coupe uses a variable-rate, speed-sensitive power assist steering system. The most assist is delivered low speeds, such as when making parking maneuvers. It then tapers off as speeds increase to return good road feel.

Brakes

Four-wheel disc brakes with power assist are standard on all Coupe models. The front ventilated discs measure 11.1 inches and the solid rear rotors are 10.2 inches. The L and LS models come equipped with Honda's own anti-lock braking system. The anti-locking system prevents the tires from locking up under severe or panic stops and maintains steering control. The low-profile P205/60R15 radial tires also help the Coupe stop from 60 miles per hour in 129 feet. Overall braking is excellent.

Ride Quality

With nearly the same length wheelbase as with the Sedan, the Coupe exhibits excellent ride quality with its slightly firm suspension and supple and well-controlled ride. The ride quality is enhanced by the strong and structurally stiff steel unit body. The oversized 15-inch wheels and tires also help to soak up the bumps. The Coupe's smooth ride makes it an excellent tourer, and an excellent choice for taking a long trip.

INTERIOR

The interior of every Coupe includes an adjustable steering column, clock, center console, illuminated vanity mirrors, cruise control, power door locks, power windows, power outside mirrors, electric moonroof and AM/FM stereo with cassette. The L models add a power adjustable driver's seat with memory and optional leather upholstery. The flagship LS model receives a full leather interior, Bose speakers and a burled walnut center console.

From the driver's seat, the Coupe has a clear and well-laid out instrument panel. The speedometer and tachometer dominate and the instrument cluster includes a combined water temperature and fuel level gauge. The cruise control has a main switch on the dash and a remote control conveniently mounted on the steering wheel.

The front bucket seats provide good room and the rear seat can accommodate adults. Overall, the interior is clean, simple and functional.

SUMMARY

The 1989 Acura Legend Coupe is the sports coupe of choice in the less than $20,000 bracket. It comes with long-legged cruising comfort, quick acceleration and excellent handling.

The Coupe also offers three distinct models of different equipment levels, but even the standard model is well equipped with air conditioning, power windows and cruise control.

Unlike many other sports coupes, the Coupe is a true four-passenger car. It's practicality includes low-maintenance and Honda's reputation for reliability, durability and quality. Acura also took top honors in the J.D. Power and Associates "Consumer Satisfaction" survey in 1987, 1988, 1989 and 1990.

1989 ACURA LEGEND COUPE

ASSETS	DEBITS
Very smooth, powerful engine	Plain interior
Good rear seat room	Limited front seat headroom
Anti-locking brakes	
Airbag on LS model	

HOW THE RUNNERS-UP PLACED
FOLLOWING THE ACURA LEGEND COUPE

2nd PLACE...1991 Volkswagen Corrado
A modern sport coupe with surprising rear seat room. The supercharged four lacks the low-end power of the Legend Coupe.

3rd PLACE...1991 Honda Prelude Si
Shares the same automaker as the Legend Coupe, but is definitely a step

down, especially when comparing its four-cylinder engine to the Legend's ultra-smooth and powerful six.

A CLOSER LOOK AT THE 1989 ACURA LEGEND COUPE

SPECIFICATIONS:	Front engine, front-wheel drive, two-door coupe.
ENGINE:	V-6
DISPLACEMENT:	2.7 liter
HORSEPOWER:	160 @ 5,900 RPM
TORQUE:	162 foot-pounds @ 4,500 RPM
INDUCTION SYSTEM:	Electronic fuel injection
RECOMMENDED FUEL:	Unleaded regular
DRIVETRAIN:	Five-speed manual
FRONT SUSPENSION:	Independent double wishbone with coil springs, gas-pressurized shocks and anti-roll bar
REAR SUSPENSION:	Independent double wishbone with coil springs, gas-pressurized shocks and anti-roll bar
STEERING TYPE:	Variable-ratio, power assisted rack-and-pinion
TURNING CIRCLE (CURB-TO-CURB):	36.5 feet
BRAKE TYPE:	Power-assisted front and rear disc with anti-lock braking system
TIRE TYPE AND SIZE:	P205/60R15
WHEELBASE:	106.5 in.
LENGTH:	188.0 in.
WIDTH:	68.7 in.
HEIGHT:	53.9 in.
CURB WEIGHT:	3,220 pounds
TRUNK CARGO VOLUME:	22-cubic feet
ACCELERATION, 0-60 MPH:	7.7 seconds
FUEL CONSUMPTION:	18-22 miles per gallon

THE BEST SPORTS COUPE
Price Range: Under $30,000

The essence here is luxury and status in a sporting platform that offers effortless performance and handling.

THE CONTENDERS*	WHOLESALE	RETAIL
1989 Cadillac Allante	$22,325	$25,625
1991 Buick Reatta Convertible	$21,000	$25,000
1991 Chrysler TC Maserati	$22,000	$26,000

*Prices of Contenders are base prices which may vary in range from those of the winning model.

The Winner

1989 CADILLAC ALLANTE

If there is such a thing as a $30,000 bargain, it's the 1989 Cadillac Allante. An Allante, which retails new for nearly $60,000, is a bargain when you can pick up a two-year old model for less than half the new car price. And the '89 Allante looks exactly like the latest '92 model.

The '89 model year is a major one for the coupe/hardtop roadster, as it went from a pretender in the ultra-luxury, personal two-seater ranks to a serious player.

Other players in the less than $30,000 used car sports coupe field include the 1991 Buick Reatta Convertible and the 1991 Chrysler TC Maserati — a pair of orphans that were last produced in 1991. A natural is the Mercedes-

Benz SL series but even an '86 is beyond our price criterion.

The '91 TC was only available with a 3.0-liter Mitsubishi V-6 engine with 141 horsepower that is no match for Allante's 200 horsepower V-8. Ditto for the Reatta which only has 170 horsepower from its 3.8-liter V-6 on tap. More importantly, the Cadillac's 4.5-liter powerplant is a much more tractable unit with 270-foot pounds of torque at 3,200 rpm. The better low-end power is evident in everyday driving situations.

The Allante debuted in 1987 as a challenger to the Mercedes-Benz SEL The Allante continues to be the only automobile in the world to be built on a production line that spans two continents. Bodies are assembled and painted in Italy by famed coachmaker Pininfarina. The trimmed bodies, complete with interiors, are transported 3,300 miles on the "Allante Airbridge" — specially outfitted Boeing 747 cargo jetliners — to Cadillac's Detroit-Hamtramck Assembly Center in Michigan, where suspension and driveline components are added.

Once completed, front-wheel-drive Allantes receive even more special care. Cadillac claims the two-seater receives more extensive and rigorous testing procedures during its construction than any other car built in North America. The complex electrical and electronic systems are certified at eight different assembly stages. Each engine is tested for an extended period of time, over a wide range of speeds on a dynamometer prior to installation. Finally, every Allante is driven for 25 miles on a specially designed 2.5-mile track after it leaves the assembly line.

However, even with all this care, the Allante has been less than a sales success. Only 1,651 Allantes were sold in '87, approximately 3,500 each year of '88 and '89.

The early Allantes were beautiful, but did not have the performance to match the competition in the marketplace. But the depreciation on the Allante's price has been much higher than warranted. Thus, it's a real bargain compared to the Buick Reatta Convertible.

With the '89 model, Cadillac took serious strides toward correcting any deficiencies. A new 4.5-liter V-8 engine developing 200 horsepower replaced the original 4.1-liter, 170-horsepower unit. With its new muscle, the Allante's performance jumped from adequate to brisk. The 0-60 mph sprint halts the stopwatch at just 8.3 seconds and top speed is a healthy 135 mph. World class numbers for a car trying to be world class.

Cadillac did not stop at the engine compartment. The Allante chassis was refined to match the higher performance potential. Changes include a stronger automatic transaxle, larger 16-inch wheels and tires, three-mode automatically adjustable suspension system and variable-assist power steering. Additional refinements include softer leather seating and door panels, a sophisticated theft-deterrent system, engine oil life indicator, central door unlocking from the trunk, and express-down windows.

When you buy an Allante, you get all the toys — power windows, door locks, cruise control, Bosch III ABS anti-lock brakes etc... The only option is a cellular telephone.

The Allante is a car with exotic Italian looks, but without the special care and feeding many exotics demand. It is a car that can easily be driven every day. Any and all problems can be corrected at the nearest Cadillac dealership for much less than it would cost to service a Mercedes. Cadillac also offers a roadside emergency service for all years and models of Cadillacs.

Size, Comfort and Style

The wide 60-inch front and rear track give the Allante a solid and stable foundation and a broad stance. The car's short deck, long hood proportions are well balanced over the 99.4-inch wheelbase and 178.6-inch length.

When the original Allante debuted in 1987, many automotive observers were surprised Pininfarina did not opt for a bolder design. However, the test of time has proven the Italian coachmaker was correct in understating the Allante styling. The sculptured aluminum body continues to look fresh and clean, well into its fifth season.

The timeless look also is a great benefit for used car buyers. Not even an

Allante expert can pick an '87 from a '92 from ten paces. The body structure should be able to last as long as the styling with its body panels constructed from either aluminum or two-sided galvanized steel. It is good looking and built to stay that way.

The clean lines have a drag coefficient of just 0.35, which improves efficiency and also keeps the wind noise down. The aerodynamics have been tuned to allow normal conversation with the top down at 55 mph.

The Allante can be driven in three configurations — hardtop, soft top and convertible. Two people can easily remove the 58-pound aluminum hardtop. The soft top features glass rear and quarter windows.

The comfort department also is aided by a new for '89 speed dependent dampening suspension system. The suspension dampening automatically shifts from three modes, allowing a soft ride at low speeds and a firmer, more controlled ride at higher speeds.

ENGINE AND DRIVETRAIN

The front-wheel-drive luxury tourer features a transverse-mounted V-8 engine. For '89 the aluminum powerplant received a 4mm increase in bore to increase the displacement from 4.1-liters to 4.5 liters.

In addition to the cubic inch gain, the engine benefits from new cylinder heads, a higher 9.0:1 compression ratio, redesigned air cleaner, throttle body and freer-flowing exhaust. All the modifications add up to 200 horsepower at 4,400 rpm and 270 foot-pounds of torque at 3,200 rpm — increases of 17 and 13 percent, respectively, over the prior year's engine. The increases even feel larger from behind the steering wheel. Throttle response is instantaneous.

Contributing to the Allante's new jump off the line is a change in the final drive ratio from 2.95:1 to 3.21:1. The THM F7 four-speed automatic transaxle, gears and clutch have been reinforced to match output of the new engine.

Handling

More than just a two-seat

luxury car, the Allante posts impressive sports car figures when it comes to the handling department. The Allante generates a maximum lateral acceleration of 0.85 on a skid pad. The heart of the Allante's excellent handling qualities is its new dependent dampening system. The system is made up of Delco deflected-disc shock absorbers that have three distinct dampening curves. The system automatically shifts among compliant, normal and firm modes according to speed. This allows a luxury-car ride at low speeds and high-speed agility and stability. In addition, anti-dive and anti-lift qualities keep the car balanced during hard braking and acceleration.

The power steering also is speed dependent. The variable-assist rack-and-pinion power steering provides generous power assistance at low speeds to minimize steering effort during parking and other low-speed maneuvers. At higher speeds, it gradually reduces the level of assistance to improve road feel and stability.

For '89, Cadillac went "plus 1" in its wheel and tire combination for the Allante. The wheel and tire size was increased one-inch in diameter to 16 inches. The specially engineered P225/55VR16 Goodyear Eagle VL tires, mounted on 16-inch by 7-inch forged aluminum wheels, offer better traction and handling.

The plus 1 wheel and tires allow for a lower profile and a shorter tire wall that respond more quickly to steering inputs. Cadillac and Goodyear engineers were able to achieve an excellent compromise between ride, comfort and handling with the 55-series tires.

Brakes

The Allante's braking system is strictly world class. The four-wheel disc setup includes 10.3-inch vented front discs and 10.0-inch solid rear discs. The sophisticated Bosch III anti-lock braking system gives the driver critical steering control under hard braking or slippery road conditions.

The powerful brakes are assisted by the dependent dampening system that greatly reduces front-end dive and rear lift during emergency-type stops. The grippy Goodyears contribute to the overall excellent braking. The braking action is near ideal and linear — the harder to press the brake pedal, the quicker the Allante stops. The brakes are easily up to the increase in the Allante's horsepower and 135 mph top speed.

Ride Quality

The ride quality is excellent thanks to the variable dampening suspension system and the solid platform. Though a convertible, the Allante with its top down has no detectible cowl shake over railroad tracks or bumps.

The suspension system gives the Allante the ride of a Cadillac sedan around town, but without any floating sensation when speeds increase. The Goodyear Eagle VL's also are very compliant for such low-profile tires. With the Allante, bumps are heard, not felt, as the suspension and tires soak up irregularities.

INTERIOR

Cadillac's continued refinement to the Allante can also be seen and felt in the interior. For '89, softer Cogolo leather covers the roadster's 10-way power adjustable Recaro seats. The foam and stitching were also redesigned to improve seat appearance and comfort. The Recaro seats, renowned for their proper lumbar and thigh support, live up to their reputation. Softer materials also are used throughout the passenger compartment, including the instrument panel, door armrests and upper door panels.

Unlike most sports coupes, the Allante has a spacious interior with plenty of room for passengers. A brief case, small bags and other incidentals can be stored behind the seats.

The instrument panel is a mix of traditional analog and digital instrument clusters. The electronic analog speedometer is accurate within 0.5 mph at 80 mph.

A driver information center is found in the center console and provides diagnostic feedback about the mechanical systems and functions as a trip computer. The system controls the climate and Delco-Bose symphony sound system. It is comprehensive, but takes getting used to.

New on the '89 Allante is an oil-life indicator. Similar to the unit found on BMWs, the system calculates oil life based on miles driven and the frequency and duration of trips. The Allante also is equipped with General

Motors' personalized automotive security system that uses coded resistors in the ignition key and lock to verify authorized operation.

The power windows have an express-down feature that fully lowers the window with just one brief touch. The central locking system allows the trunk to be unlocked with one turn of the key and the doors with a second turn of the key.

SUMMARY

The '89 Cadillac Allante is a four-wheel bargain in the personal luxury sports coupe field. A late-model Allante can be purchased for far less than its new price. It offers world class performance, creature comforts and status at much less than its rivals.

Low production numbers also have made the Allante an exclusive vehicle that is just not found around every corner. The understated Pininfarina body style has a timeless quality that has weathered time well and is nearly identical to the latest models.

The Chrysler TC Maserati basically is the Allante concept — Italian body with American mechanicals — but has fallen short. Even with the smooth Mitsubishi V-6, the poor-selling TC proved a V-8 is needed to compete at this price and luxury level.

1989 CADILLAC ALLANTE

ASSETS	DEBITS
Pininfarina design	Driver information center confusing
Anti-lock rear brakes	Soft top difficult to operate
200 horsepower V-8	Recaro interior

HOW THE RUNNERS-UP PLACED
FOLLOWING THE CADILLAC ALLANTE

2nd PLACE...1991 Buick Reatta Convertible

The '91 model benefited from refinements following four years of production, but soft sales killed it. Resale value and future parts and services needs are questionable.

3rd PLACE... 1991 Chrysler TC Maserati

No longer produced, resale value and future parts and service needs are questionable.

A CLOSER LOOK AT THE 1989 CADILLAC ALLANTE

SPECIFICATIONS:	Front engine, front-wheel drive, two-door roadster with hardtop.
ENGINE:	V-8
DISPLACEMENT:	4.5 liter
HORSEPOWER:	200 @ 4,400 RPM
TORQUE:	270 foot-pounds @ 3,200 RPM
INDUCTION SYSTEM:	Sequential multi-port fuel injection
RECOMMENDED FUEL:	Unleaded regular
DRIVETRAIN:	Four-speed automatic
FRONT SUSPENSION:	Independent strut with coil springs
REAR SUSPENSION:	Independent with coil springs
STEERING TYPE:	Power-assisted rack-and-pinion
TURNING CIRCLE (CURB-TO-CURB):	36 feet
BRAKE TYPE:	Power-assisted front disc/rear disc Bosch III Anti-Lock
TIRE TYPE AND SIZE:	P225/55R16
WHEELBASE:	99.4 in.
LENGTH:	178.6 in.
WIDTH:	73.5 in.
HEIGHT:	52.2 in.
CURB WEIGHT:	3,491 pounds
TRUNK CARGO VOLUME:	16.2 cubic feet
ACCELERATION, 0-60 MPH:	8.3 seconds
FUEL CONSUMPTION:	15-22 miles per gallon

BEST SPORTS COUPE
Price Range: Over $30,000

For more than $30,000 the ideal sports coupe must do more than just accelerate briskly, stop quickly and corner-like on rails. It must also have superior quality, build and exude status, superior styling and class.

THE CONTENDERS*	WHOLESALE	RETAIL
1989 BMW 635CSi	$26,750	$30,050
1990 Mercedes-Benz 560SEC . . .	$49,200	$54,225
1989 Porsche 928S 4	$36,300	$40,300

*Prices of Contenders are base prices which may vary in range from those of the winning model.

The Winner

1989 BMW 635CSi

Sports coupes in the rarified "cost is no object" category are much more than just mere mortal automobiles and much more than a handful of performance figures from a stopwatch or a skidpad.

These ultra sports coupes go beyond being a robotic assemblage of metal, plastic and rubber. They have soul. They live and breathe and have distinct personalities.

Soul and personality are earned from their heritage, elegant styling and hand-built quality that puts a little of the craftsman into each car.

The best sports coupe over $30,000 is the 1989 BMW 635CSi. The 635CSi is the ultimate car from the makers of "Ultimate Driving Machines."

In the Olympics of sports coupes, the Mercedes-Benz 560SEC has a larger interior, especially for rear passengers and the Porsche 928S4 is quicker and faster than the BMW. However, in this heady competition, the 635CSi is the winner of the decathlon. An athletic and graceful automobile that blends luxury, performance and handling in an elegant sports coupe package that many have called classic.

However, the overused term "classic" properly describes the 635CSi. This Teutonic supercar was retired after the '89 model year and finally replaced by the BMW 850i in 1991.

The 850i, powered by a 5-liter V-12 engine, has a suggested retail price of nearly $80,000. Add to that atmospheric figure, federal gas guzzler and luxury taxes and we're talking about a serious chunk of money. Meanwhile, a used '89 635CSi can be purchased for between $28,700 and $32,050 and surrenders absolutely nothing to the 850i when it comes to prestige, status and elegance.

In addition, an '89 635CSi should retain more of its purchase price value than the newer sports coupe. As the last of the 1977-89 series of BMW 6-Series sports coupes, the 635CSi is a true special-interest vehicle and possibly could, in time, appreciate in value. They don't make them like that any more and the styling is timeless.

The BMW 6-Series sports coupes debuted on U.S. shores in 1977 as the 630CSi. The first numeral in the name signified the series and the following two digits, the displacement of the engine. Thus, the 630CSi was powered by a 3.0-liter version of what has been called the most sophisticated inline six in the world.

The following year brought the 633CSi, with its slightly larger 3.3-liter engine that improved the car's acceleration and driveability. In 1986, the engine displacement jumped to 3.5-liters and brought the designation to 635CSi.

In 1987, the 635CSi was joined by a pair of running mates; the L6 and the M6. Basically, the L6 was the BMW sports coupe clothed with an even more luxurious interior, automatic transmission and a suspension tuned for a softer ride.

The M6 was a product of BMW's Motorsports Division and was tuned and outfitted for an even higher level of performance. In the M6, the BMW six-engine is massaged with a four-valve cylinder head and other modifications to produce 256 horsepower and performance numbers of 6.8 seconds from 0-60 miles per hour and a top speed of 156 mph. The M6, which has a sports suspension package to match its high-revving engine, can easily be identified by its wider tires, front and rear spoilers and "M" badging.

The L6 was dropped after its initial year and the M6 was last imported to American in 1988. The '89 635CSi is a true blend of both the L6 and the M6. The L6 and M6 were narrower-focused vehicles and their rarity should add to their long-term value. The '87 L6 has a used car value range of about $22,000. Used prices for the '87-'88 M6 go from $27,000 to $31,000.

Size, Comfort and Style

The 635CSi is solidly constructed with its curb weight of 3,530 pounds distributed over its 103.3-inch wheelbase and 189.6-inch overall length. The 635CSi drives and feels behind the wheel like a much smaller car. This is due to its nimble handling, excellent road feel and the large glass area that gives the driver an excellent view of the road and other vehicles.

The 635CSi provides luxury car comfort with many opulent features that include hand-stitched Nappa leather interior, velour carpeting, 10-way power seats with memory, electric windows and electronic cruise control. Just set the cruise control, put in your favorite CD and hit the road. The 635CSi has long-legs and is a true grand touring vehicle.

Seating comfort is excellent for the front passengers and like many sports coupes, tight for the rear adult passengers. The rear passengers do have the comfort advantage of an independent rear air conditioner.

The styling theme of the 635CSi was essentially carried over from the earlier 2800CSi and 3.0 CSi models. The BMW family resemblance is threaded through the 2800CSi on to the 850i. By maintaining the same styling theme, the cars do not look outmoded. This is a large reason why BMW automobiles have the reputation for high-resale value.

To be successful with the same basic design year after year, you have to start with a winner. BMW designers penned the 635CSi with a classically elegant, yet sporty, body design. The styling with its large greenhouse, long hood and short deck proportions have been widely copied. The original Acura Legend Coupe owes much to the 635CSi and there is no mistaking the origins of the profile of the latest Ford Thunderbird.

However, the clones have not captured the light, airy elegance of the BMW design and they definitely do not have the 635CSi's timeless appeal.

ENGINE AND DRIVETRAIN

The 635CSi is powered by a 3.5-liter, single-overhead cam, inline six that delivers 208 horsepower at 5,700 rpm. The maximum 225 foot-pounds of torque is generated at 4,000 rpm.

Called by enthusiasts for years the most sophisticated inline six in the world, the big six has kept pace with modern developments. Induction is by Bosch Motronic electronic fuel injection. The induction, electronic breakerless ignition and emission controls are controlled by a Digital Motor Electronics engine-management system that allows the use of unleaded regular gasoline. A stainless steel exhaust system ensures longevity.

The 3.5-liter unit is known for its durability and reliability. The basic

powerplant was used in many CSi-based race cars, including twin-turbocharged racers that contested 24-hour endurance races at LeMans, France and Daytona.

Engine accessibility is good, with the front-hinged hood opening up and out of the way. A nice touch is how the hood is closed without the usual dropping or slamming. To close the 635CSi hood, the hood is gently set down on the body and the final closure is done inside the passenger compartment by pulling back the hood open-close lever.

The 635CSi is available with either a five-speed manual Getrag transmission or a four-speed ZF automatic transmission. The manual unit has a 3.64:1 final drive ratio and is positive-shifting. With the manual transmission, the 635CSi is conservatively rated by the factory to sprint from 0-60 miles per hour in 7.9 seconds and have a top speed of 138. Fuel economy, as estimated by the EPA, is 15 miles per gallon city and 23 mpg highway.

The no-charge automatic has a torque converter and torque-converter lockup clutch that is electronically controlled. The final drive ratio with the automatic is 3.91:1. The higher final drive ratio gives an automatic straight line performance that rivals the manually transmissioned model. EPA numbers for the automatic are 15 mpg city and 19 mpg highway.

If the 635CSi does not have enough performance for you, seek out the much more potent M6 model.

HANDLING

If you advertise your cars as "The Ultimate Driving Machine" you better be able to back it up, and BMW does. By ultimate driving, BMW is not talking about g's pulled on the skidpad or sped through a slalom. Ultimate driving to BMW is the vehicle's ability to instantly respond and give input and feedback on vehicle dynamics and road conditions.

BMW's philosophy in vehicle dynamics is "the driver is a fully functional part of the car itself, the human part of the equation which completes the car's mechanical system."

Much of BMW's reputation for incredible handling and alive response was created by the 6-series sports coupes. The '89 635CSi takes that even further with new Servotronic power steering, which replaces the former engine-speed controlled power assist with electronically controlled car-speed sensitive assist. The new system gives a lighter steering effort for parking and low-speed maneuvering with the same firm road feel BMW drivers expect.

The 635CSi front suspension consists of MacPherson struts, double-pivot lower A-arms, coil springs, twin-tube gas-pressurized shock absorbers and an anti-roll bar. The rear suspension utilizes semi-trailing arms, coil springs, gas-pressurized shock absorbers, an anti-roll bar and a self-leveling system.

Brakes

The 635CSi uses huge 11.2-inch ventilated front discs, teamed with 11.2-inch rear discs. The power assist activates hydraulic circuits which are divided diagonally. An anti-lock braking system ensures quick and sure stops. Anti-lock brakes prevent the tires from locking and losing traction no matter the surface or condition and maintains steering control.

Ride Quality

BMW's proven method for both a good ride and high-performance handling has been a relatively soft spring with firm shock absorbers, anti-roll bars and a solid chassis. The soft spring is effective because of the sports coupe's generous suspension travel. Ride quality is excellent — blasting the autobahn at 135 miles per hour or cruising a U.S. interstate at 60 mph.

The excellently controlled suspension and independent action allows the 635CSi to handle ruts and bumps, even those in the middle of a turn that unbalance lesser cars.

INTERIOR

The 635CSi has four-place seating, but is most inviting for the two front passengers. The front seats have 10-way power adjustments including head restraints. The driver's side seat has three memory settings.

The interior is beautifully finished with hand-stitched Nappa leather upholstery covering the seats, door panels, lower dash and

console. Rich velour carpeting complements the leather surfaces.

The three-spoke, leather-covered steering wheel frames the large speedometer and tachometer in the instrument cluster. The onboard trip computer has nine functions including two with audible and visual warnings. The BMW Service Interval Indicator signals when maintenance is required by monitoring the number of cold starts and trip lengths. Vehicles making short trips and not thoroughly warming up require servicing sooner.

Other interior features include a roll-up rear sunshade, electric two-way sunroof, anti-theft AM/FM stereo with cassette, power amplifier with equalizer and eight speakers and fully finished trunk with the famous BMW drop-down tool kit. The only interior options are heated front seats and a six-disc CD player and changer.

SUMMARY

In the automotive Olympics, the BMW 635CSi is a decathlon champion. An athletic and graceful sports coupe that blends luxury, performance and handling in an elegantly-styled package that many have called classic and timeless.

The heart of the 635CSi is the famous BMW inline six, noted for its world-class smoothness, tractability, durability and reliability.

The 635CSi is a relative bargain when compared to its 850i replacement at nearly $80,000. As the final year of the 6-Series generation of sports coupes, the '89 635CSi should, in time, top even BMW's legendary tradition of high resale value.

1989 BMW 635CSi

ASSETS	DEBITS
Smooth six-cylinder engine	Small rear seat area
Timeless elegant styling	Expensive service and repair
Anti-lock braking system	
Driver's side airbag	

HOW THE RUNNERS-UP PLACED
FOLLOWING THE BMW 635CSi

2nd PLACE...1990 Mercedes-Benz 560SEC

A Powerful car that's larger than the BMW 635CSi, but priced much higher. Fuel consumption is higher than the BMW.

3rd PLACE...1989 Porsche 928S4

Thirty-two valve V-8 engine gives a performance that exceeds the BMW, but at a much higher price. Lacks the classically elegant styling of the BMW.

A CLOSER LOOK AT THE 1989 BMW 635CSi

SPECIFICATIONS:	Front engine, rear-wheel drive sports coupe.
ENGINES:	Inline six-cylinder
DISPLACEMENT:	3.5 liter
HORSEPOWER:	208 @ 5,700 RPM
TORQUE:	225-foot pounds @ 4,000 RPM
INDUCTION SYSTEM:	Electronic multiport fuel injection
RECOMMENDED FUEL:	Unleaded regular
DRIVETRAIN:	Five-speed manual
FRONT SUSPENSION:	Independent with coil springs, gas-pressurized shock absorbers, anti-roll bar
REAR SUSPENSION:	Independent with coil springs, gas-pressurized shock absorbers, anti-roll bar
STEERING TYPE:	Variable-ratio, power assisted recirculating ball
TURNING CIRCLE (CURB-TO-CURB):	37.4 feet
BRAKE TYPE:	Power-assisted front and rear discs with anti-lock braking system
TIRE TYPE AND SIZE:	P220/55VR390
WHEELBASE:	103.3 in.
LENGTH:	189.6 in.
WIDTH:	67.9 in.
HEIGHT:	53.7 in.
CURB WEIGHT:	3,530 pounds
TRUNK CARGO VOLUME:	14.6-cubic feet
ACCELERATION, 0-60 MPH:	7.9 seconds
FUEL CONSUMPTION:	15-23 miles per gallon

BEST SPORTS CAR
Price Range: Under $10,000

At under $10,000, we're looking for an affordable sports car for the "rest of us." However, there still should not be any sacrifice in the virtues that make sports cars fun to own and drive.

THE CONTENDERS*	WHOLESALE	RETAIL
1990 Honda CRX Si	$7,925	$9,200
1988 Mazda RX-7 GTU	$7,150	$8,300
1989 Toyota MR2	$7,700	$8,950

*Prices of Contenders are base prices which may vary in range from those of the winning model.

The Winner

1988 MAZDA RX-7 GTU

In the race for the best used sports car under $10,000, the 1988 Mazda RX-7 GTU takes the checkered flag first. The rotary-powered coupe slips ahead of two other Japanese sportsters — the 1989 Toyota MR2 and 1990 Honda CRX Si.

The RX-7 advantage is its ultra-reliable powertrain, race-proven chassis and a complete family of models. The Mazda sports car is available in six versions — base SE, sporting GTU, luxurious GXL, 2+2 seating, high-performance Turbo and Convertible.

The GTU model features 15-inch alloy wheels and high-performance, low-profile tires, sport-tuned suspension, sport seats, aerodynamic body pieces, limited-slip differential and body colored electric door mirrors.

The heart of the RX-7 is its unique twin-rotor Wankel engine. While Mazda first debuted the world's first mass-produced rotary automobile in 1971, it was the RX-7 that established the innovative powerplant.

The RX-2 and RX-3 sports sedans were overnight sensations when they hit the market in the early '70s. Mazda advertising focused on the engine's smoothness — "Mazdas go 'hummm'" — and the lack of connecting rods, pistons, valves and other conventional components. The Mazda rotary, which uses just a third of the number of parts compared to a piston engine.

Unfortunately, Mazda's U.S. fortunes and sales began falling in 1973 when gasoline prices soared and Mazda rotaries began showing a weakness in the critical apex seals. The energy crunch brought to surface that the rotary, which had much more performance, was not as miserly with a gallon of gasoline as other Japanese "economy" cars.

The bad apex seals, the equivalent of worn piston rings, resulted in a sea of dead or smoking Mazdas which further damaged Mazda's reputation. Mazda countered by repairing at a low cost many of the damaged units and withdrawing all new rotary offerings. Mazda then introduced its piston GLC economy car.

However, Mazda was not about to give up on the genius of Felix Wankel. Mazda would come out with another rotary-powered car, but this time it absolutely had to be right — in performance and fuel economy — or the rotary would be dead for ever.

Debuting in 1978, the '79 RX-7 was right. The new rotary engine was refined and improved with stronger seals and more efficient water and oil cooling systems. The much stronger, 100-horsepower engine was housed in a body design that featured a sloping hood with concealed headlights that flip up. The functional body was highlighted by a black bumper strip that surrounds and protects the car's midline. The package, which sold for less than $7,000, was finished off with a clear rear hatch made entirely of glass.

The RX-7 was a smash hit. Within three years, total sales topped 100,000 units. The success of the sports car brought Mazda and the rotary back into good graces.

The RX-7 received a facelift in 1981 and the second generation RX-7 was unveiled in the 1986 model year. The 1986-91 model features a body style that is reminiscent of a Porsche 944. The line up also expanded to include Convertible, Turbo and 2+2 models.

The RX-7 was even more successful, if that is possible, on the race track. A pair of unproven RX-7 race cars finished first and second in their debut in the IMSA GTU class at the 1979 24 Hours of Daytona.

RX-7 has continued to dominate the GTU racing division and has become a force in the faster IMSA GTO and Camel Light GTP class.

The zenith of Mazda rotary racing took place at the 24 Hours of LeMans. At the French classic, a four-rotor Mazda prototype entry averaged 127.6 mph in the twice around the clock race, topping favorites Mercedes-Benz, Jaguar and Porsche for the overall win.

Mazda race cars have been at their best in endurance races like Daytona and LeMans, because the rotary engine is so durable. This durability and reliability is also found in Mazda RX-7s that don't wear racing numbers.

In a survey of Mazda RX-7 repair and service shops, it was estimated that the RX-7's engine should be good for 150,000-200,000 miles before needing an overhaul. Three major reasons for the longevity are the inherent smoothness of the rotary engine; only three primary moving parts, and the external combustion design does not contaminate the oil supply with corrosive byproducts of combustion.

Size, Comfort and Style

The 1988 RX-7 is a roomy sports car for the driver and the passenger. The passenger compartment is especially good for tall drivers with its excellent legroom.

The amount of comfort of the RX-7 can be determined by the model selected. The SE features the base four-wheel-independent suspension and has compliant P185/70HR14 tires for a good ride. The GTU and Turbo have the stiffer, more sport-tuned suspensions. The GXL has an automatic adjusting suspension with two modes — normal and sport. The GXL costs about $1,000 more than the GTU.

The clean, aerodynamic shape of the RX-7 features a smoothly-rounded nose and low hoodline, a steeply raked windshield and a large, tapered rear hatchback. Retractable headlights and the compact rotary engine allow for the steep hoodline. Other exterior highlights include the fender flares at each corner that give the RX-7 a wide and aggressive stance.

The SE has a drag coefficient of 0.31, which can be lowered to 0.30 by the "aero" body pieces of the GTU model. The stylish Convertible slips through the air with a drag number of 0.33 with its cloth top up. But the convertible will cost well over $10,000.

The Convertible's power top can be positioned in three positions: fully up, half-open and fully open.

ENGINE AND DRIVETRAIN

The 1988 RX-7's two available rotary engines are the result of more than a decade of refinement. The '88 version features six-port induction, electronic fuel-injection and a microprocessor-controlled engine management system. The induction system includes what Mazda calls Dynamic Effect Intake, which tunes the intake to take advantage of the basic "surge" phenomenon peculiar to the rotary for free supercharging.

The 1.3-liter, twin-rotor engine produces 146 horsepower at 6,500 rpm and 138 foot-pounds of torque at 3,500 rpm. A five-speed manual transmission is standard, with a four-speed overdrive automatic optional. Final drive ratios for all models is 4.10:1 for the manual and 3.90:1 for the automatic. The Convertible is available only with a manual transmission.

The RX-7 Turbo utilizes a unique dual-chamber scroll turbocharger design to provide increased torque and engine response at low rpms while also delivering a turbo's traditional higher speed boost. The exhaust-driven turbocharger features primary and secondary chambers separated by an integral cast wall with an intake vacuum-activated valve to open or close the secondary chamber. At low engine speeds, the turbocharger is fed through the smaller primary opening, concentrating the exhaust gases and increasing their velocity, thus improving low-speed response and torque. The larger secondary chamber opens above 2,500 mph or under certain load conditions to allow full flow through the turbocharger for outstanding performance at higher rpms. An air-to-air intercooler is positioned directly over the intake plenum to cool and condense the incoming air.

The potent engine generates 182 horsepower at 6,500 rpm and 183 foot-pounds of torque at 3,500 rpm. The Turbo is available only with a five-speed transmission. It will cost you just under $2,000 more than the GTU.

HANDLING

The RX-7 is a great handling car that is very forgiving. It does not complain whether it is tossed around or driven smoothly. That kind of handling begins with near perfect weight distribution, which is aided by the compact and lightweight rotary engine, mounted behind the front axle center line. The unsprung weight of the car also has been greatly reduced by the use of high-strength, lightweight aluminum alloys for the front suspension A-arms, wheel hubs, differential housing and other components.

A chassis engineer will tell you that a vehicle's rear suspension design is the key to good handling. The RX-7 has a very advanced rear suspension design that Mazda calls Dynamic Tracking Suspension System (DTSS). Similar to the Porsche 928 and BMW 750 series, the Mazda system allows some rear wheel steering to enhance stability.

In low lateral force cornering, the DTSS allows the rear wheels to toe-out slightly, providing quick turn-in and response. At higher lateral force, the DTSS dials in a toe-in attitude, resulting in added stability.

Front and rear anti-roll bars and low-pressure gas-filled shock absorbers are standard on all RX-7 models. A two-mode — normal and sport — automatic adjusting suspension system is standard on the GXL model.

Brakes

More than matching the RX-7's performance and handling potential are four-wheel-disc brakes. The SE model features power-assisted ventilated front discs and solid rear discs. The GTU received larger 10.9-inch front brakes and ventilated rear disc brakes. Available on the GXL and Turbo models is an anti-lock braking system that ensures optimum braking performance and allows the driver to maintain steering control during panic stops or stops in slippery conditions.

Ride Quality

If a comfortable ride is a high priority, opt for the GXL model with its automatic adjusting suspension with two modes — normal and sport. The next choice would be the base SE model with its more compliant P185/70HR14 tires and its softer, base suspension.

The GTU and Turbo models have sport-tuned suspensions that give a more responsive, but firmer ride. Also stiffening up the ride are the P205/60VR15 tires on the GTU and the Turbo's P205/55VR16 tires.

INTERIOR

Behind the three-spoke, leather-wrapped steering wheel, the driver can easily read the large, center-mounted analog tachometer, speedometer and pertinent gauges. A high-mounted panel above the center console includes a digital clock and warning lights.

There is room to stretch out in the RX-7's supportive bucket seats. Seat materials include velour upholstery on the SE, twill upholstery sport seats on the GTU and Turbo, herringbone velour on the Convertible and velour or optional leather on the GXL.

The generous cargo area under the glass hatchback includes a pair

of lockable storage boxes. On the SE and GXL, the storage boxes can be substituted for 2+2 jump seats. As with most 2+2 models, the seating area is best for small children and the seat backs tumble forward to increase the cargo space.

Standard on all RX-7 models are remote hatch/trunk and fuel filler releases, AM/FM stereo with cassette deck and four speakers, power antenna, digital clock, theft alarm, and center console with armrest. The luxury GXL standard equipment includes an electric sunroof, rear window wiper/washer, power windows, cruise control, and air conditioning.

SUMMARY

The 1988 Mazda RX-7 GTU, an excellent value when new, is an excellent value in the used car market. Plenty of room for two passengers and all their luggage for a long weekend and more. The handling is crisp and well balanced. The durability and reliability of the smooth rotary engine is second to none and proven at race tracks around the world.

The GTU is the best handling RX-7 and costs thousands less than the similar looking Turbo model. The GTU engine is less complicated than the Turbo and should generally be more reliable. The RX-7 lineup also gives you the option of a true convertible version, but the convertible is out of this price range.

1988 MAZDA RX-7 GTU

ASSETS	DEBITS
Award-winning design	Insurance surcharge
Four-wheel disc brakes	
Reliable rotary engine	
Excellent handling	

HOW THE RUNNERS-UP PLACED
FOLLOWING THE MAZDA RX-7 GTU
2nd PLACE...1989 Toyota MR2

Great handling with its mid-engine layout. Interior and luggage space very limited compared to the RX-7.

3rd PLACE...1990 Honda CRX Si
Good performance and excellent fuel economy. Interior space limited, front-wheel-drive not as sporting as the RX-7.

A CLOSER LOOK AT THE 1988 MAZDA RX-7 GTU

SPECIFICATIONS:	Front engine, rear-wheel drive, two-door sports car. Options include turbocharged, convertible and 2+2 versions.
ENGINE:	Twin rotor
DISPLACEMENT:	1.3 liter
HORSEPOWER:	146 @ 6,500 RPM
TORQUE:	138 foot-pounds @ 3,500 RPM
INDUCTION SYSTEM:	Electronic fuel injection
RECOMMENDED FUEL:	Unleaded regular
DRIVETRAIN:	Five-speed manual
FRONT SUSPENSION:	Independent strut-type with coil springs, stabilizer bar
REAR SUSPENSION:	Independent, multi-link and stabilizer bar
STEERING TYPE:	Rack-and-pinion
TURNING CIRCLE (CURB-TO-CURB):	32.2 feet
BRAKE TYPE:	Power-assisted front disc/rear disc
TIRE TYPE AND SIZE:	P205/60VR15
WHEELBASE:	95.7 in.
LENGTH:	168.9 in.
WIDTH:	66.5 in.
HEIGHT:	49.8 in.
CURB WEIGHT:	2,720 pounds
TRUNK CARGO VOLUME:	Approximately 17 cubic feet
ACCELERATION, 0-60 MPH:	8.0 seconds
FUEL CONSUMPTION:	17-24 miles per gallon

BEST SPORTS CAR
Price Range: Under $15,000

The emphasis is on a package that provides a driver and his passenger world-class acceleration, handling, overall performance and most important, driving pleasure.

THE CONTENDERS*	WHOLESALE	RETAIL
1986 Chevrolet Corvette	$9,950	$11,450
1989 Nissan 300ZX Turbo	$11,975	$13,825
1987 Porsche 944S	$10,275	$11,850

*Prices of Contenders are base prices which may vary in range from those of the winning model.

The Winner

1987 PORSCHE 944S

Sports cars are not meant to be practical. The basic concept calls for a vehicle that can transport two passengers from point A to point B in the least amount of time. With sports cars, the quickest route between point A and B is not necessarily a straight line — true sports cars love curves and corners and boast handling that can straighten out the winding road.

The latest sports car can do all of the above, while providing creature comforts, fuel efficiency and most important, driving pleasure.

The three contenders for Best Sports Car under $15,000 are an international group, representing the United States, Japan and Germany. To achieve nearly the same goals, each automobile and its manufacturer chose a different route.

The heart of the Chevrolet Corvette is a thumping 5.7-liter all-American V-8 and a chassis capable of putting up high cornering figures. The Nissan 300ZX Turbo utilizes an exhaust-driven supercharger to boost horsepower and performance out of a dated Japanese chassis. The Teutonic Porsche 944S is our No. 1 choice for this price and vehicle category because it is the best all-around in speed, power, fuel economy, braking and handling.

Since it's 1983 model year debut, the Porsche 944 has been one of the best handling cars on the road. The 944's advantage is largely due to its rear-mounted transaxle that results in an optimum 49 percent front and 51 percent rear weight distribution. What it lacked in acceleration and speed, the 944 made up with its superior handling and massive four-wheel disc brakes.

However, in 1987 Porsche made up for the horsepower deficiency with a new 16-valve cylinder head for the 2.5-liter four-cylinder engine. The four-valve head was tested earlier in a 944 race car that won its class at the famed 24-Hours of LeMans endurance race. With the deeper breathing head, horsepower jumped from 147 to 188. Torque is up 21 percent over the two-valve 944 engine — 170 foot-pounds from 140.

The new underhood power translates on the more useable and wider powerband. According to Porsche figures, the '87 Porsche 944S stops the clocks at 7.7 seconds for the 0-60 mph sprint and has a top speed of 142 mph. Amazingly, fuel economy is nearly the same as the less powerful, two-valve engine. The '87 EPA rating for the 944S is 19 miles per gallon city and 26 mpg in the highway mode.

The new powerplant is wrapped in solid body structure with extremely high-torsional strength. The stiff platform anchors the four-wheel independent suspension and powerful disc brakes at each corner.

In 1987 the Porsche 944S had a suggested manufacturer's price of $30,850. The 944S was the best value among the three 944 offerings that year which included the $27,840 944 and the $36,300 944 Turbo.

With its current used car wholesale price of $10,275 and average retail of $11,850, the '87 944S is a tremendous bargain and about the lowest entry fee to experience the Porsche mystique.

A large part of that mystique is Porsche's racing heritage. For more than

40 years, the German automaker has used racing to refine and develop its road-going cars. The most successful marque in racing history, Porsches are established winners in endurance sports car racing, international pro rallying, CART Indy cars and even Formula One.

It is not the glory of victories that Porsche is after, instead the Zuffenhausen firm uses its racing experience to develop new ideas and concepts. The four-valve cylinder head of the 944S was developed from the 956 World Endurance Championship racer. Porsche also uses auto racing to motivate and provide its engineers with a unique form of training.

For 1992, the 944 series has evolved into the 968, that utilizes the same basic platform with styling accents from the flagship 928. The 3.0-liter 968 has a suggested retail price of $39,850.

Used car buyers purchasing a 944S from an authorized Porsche dealer may qualify for a one-year, limited warranty. Qualifying vehicles are 1986 and later with up to 125,000 miles and must pass a stringent 100-plus item inspection. The warranty is in addition to any remaining new car limited warranty.

More than the typical powertrain warranty, the Porsche warranty covers — at no extra charge — all major engine components and systems, the complete transmission, all electric motors, all electrical control units, all pumps such as fuel pumps, air conditioning compressors and power steering pumps and many other components. The transferable warranty also includes one year of

Porsche's roadside emergency assistance program.

Size, Comfort and Style

The sleek 944S body is carried over a 94.49-inch wheelbase and an overall length of 168.9 inches. Workmanship and quality throughout is excellent. The relatively short wheelbase allows the 944S to have a tight 33.8-foot turning circles. Making a "U" turn in the middle of a street is no problem.

The very solid package houses a roomy interior with bucket seats for the front passengers and a pair of occasional folding rear jump seats. The rear seating area is for small children and is best used with the seat backs folded forward for luggage and packages.

A true grand touring machine, the 944S has the capacity to handle all the luggage, cargo and needs for two travelers taking an extended trip. Trunk cargo volume of the hatchback is 10.4-cubic feet and grows to an impressive 18.3-cubic feet when the rear jump seatbacks are tumbled forward.

Porsche designers worked wonders with the 944 styling, which is based on the earlier 924 model. Porsche improved the car's aggressiveness tenfold with IMSA racing inspired flared fenders and larger tires and wheels. The makeover and the Porsche engine replacing the 924's Audi unit, gives the 944S a true Porsche identity.

A long list of standard creature comforts include air conditioning, power windows, sunroof and AM/FM stereo with cassette.

ENGINE AND DRIVETRAIN

The aluminum-block 944S engine is a sophisticated unit that shares many components and engineering features with the flagship Porsche 928S 4. The 944S unit has been described as basically one bank of the 928S 4's V-8 engine.

The 2.5-liter, four-cylinder engine is rated at 188 horsepower at 6,000 rpm and 170 foot-pounds of torque at 4,300 rpm. The advanced four-valve per cylinder technology — two intake and two exhaust valves — improves the fill rate and mixing for fuel and

air in the combustion chamber. The design tolerates an extremely high compression ratio of 10.9:1. Premium unleaded gasoline is required.

To handle the wide range of quality among unleaded fuels, three electronic sensors monitor the engine. Two knock sensors attach at the crankcase and a third sensor is connected to the camshaft drive wheel. These adjust the engine to operate at all times near, but not over the line where premature combustion — knock — cause power loss and damage.

The five-speed manual transmission was strengthened to handle the increased power with the 944S. The transmission is part of a rear-mounted transaxle. By mounting the transmission at the rear of the car, the unit balances the weight of the front engine to enhance the distribution of weight.

The front-mounted engine and rear-mounted transmission are bolted together with a connection pipe to make up a rigid drive unit. The rigid mounting also enhances the shifting action.

The five-speed transmission's gear ratios are well matched to the 944S engine's powerband. Fifth gear is an overdriven 0.829. The final drive ratio is 3.89:1. A limited-slip differential and automatic transmission are optional. The automatic is a three-speed unit with a final drive ratio of 3.455:1. Performance falls off only slightly with the automatic — just .2 seconds slower to 60 mph than the manual unit.

HANDLING

The Porsche 944S has been described by car buff magazines to be the best handling car. Enough said.

The world-class handling comes from Porsche's racing heritage that results in a neutral-handling car. That balance comes from the 49/51 weight distribution and optimum tires and wheels. The tire sizes have been staggered front to back. The rubber are P205/55R16, with the rear taking a larger P225/50R16.

The fully independent suspension and staggered tires give the 944S impeccable road manners. The 944S has tremendous cornering and handling limits that most drivers will never reach. At speed, the 944S has a slight understeering attitude, that a skilled driver can neutralize with the right steering and throttle inputs. The responsive rack-and-pinion steering has just the right power assist and gives excellent feedback on what the tires are doing.

Brakes

The 944S has a massive vented disc brake at each corner. The front units have a diameter of 11.12 inches and the rear 11.38. The brake pedal feel is excellent and the action linear — the harder you press, the quicker the car stops. The excellent brakes are assisted by the 16-inch high-performance tires that put a lot of rubber on the road. The 944 can stop from 60 mph in 138 feet.

The 944S power-assisted braking system can only be improved by the optional anti-lock braking system. With ABS, tire lockup and directional control is maintained during panic stop situations and braking in slippery conditions.

Ride Quality

While the 944S is a sports car and not a luxury tourer, it exhibits a firm, but not harsh ride. The sophisticated suspension is not unsettled by a bump in the middle of the road.

The ride is not luxury car soft, but solid and well controlled. The solid construction and strength of the body structure adds to the ride quality. The supportive bucket seats are comfortable for short and long trips. Overall, the 944S is a good compromise between high-performance handling and highway touring.

INTERIOR

The first time you sit in the driver's seat of the 944S you know it was meant for driving. In Porsche tradition, a large speedometer and tachometer dominate the instrument panel. The two gauges are easily seen through the thick, leather-wrapped, four-spoke steering wheel.

The interior is typical of Porsches and other German cars — simple, functional and lacking frills. The bucket seats give good support and are comfortable. Optional seats are available with electric fore and aft, height and back adjustments.

Airbags for both driver and front-seat passenger were optional on the '87 944S and 944. The passive restraints are standard on the 944 Turbo.

There is plenty of room for two passengers and their luggage. The rear jump seats, which have independent folding backrests, truly are occasional seats and are best for small children and packages or luggage.

An AM/FM stereo with cassette is standard with a premium Blaupunkt BEA 80 booster/equalizer with ten built-in speakers optional.

SUMMARY

The 1987 Porsche 944S is the best balanced of the entire 944 series, in price, value and performance. The addition of the potent 16-valve engine gives the 944S the acceleration and speed to match the always incredible handling chassis.

Porsches have proven themselves to be of high-quality construction, reliable and long lasting. Many Porsche owners are fanatical about their cars and maintain and service them above and beyond the factory recommendations. Well-maintained Porsches are not an exception. Porsche Clubs throughout the world also help to keep the value, exclusiveness and mystique of the marque.

The factory-backed, one-year warranty with used Porsches purchased from authorized Porsche dealerships is another alternative when looking to buy a 944S.

1987 PORSCHE 944S

ASSETS	DEBITS
Strong 16-valve engine	Service and replacement part
Great handling	costs high
High quality	Insurance surcharge
ABS brakes and airbags available	

HOW THE RUNNERS-UP PLACED
FOLLOWING THE PORSCHE 944S

2nd PLACE...The 1986 Chevrolet Corvette

Impressive performance numbers, but lacks everyday comfort and refinement.

3rd PLACE...The 1989 Nissan 300ZX Turbo
The final year of a tired design. The all-new 1990 model is a tremendous improvement.

A CLOSER LOOK AT THE 1987 PORSCHE 944S

SPECIFICATIONS:	Front engine, two-wheel drive, two-door sports car. Also available in eight-valve 944 and 944 Turbo versions.
ENGINE:	Four cylinder
DISPLACEMENT:	2.5 liter
HORSEPOWER:	188 @ 6,000 RPM
TORQUE:	170 foot-pounds @ 4,300 RPM
INDUCTION SYSTEM:	DME fuel injection
RECOMMENDED FUEL:	Unleaded premium
DRIVETRAIN:	Five-speed manual transaxle
FRONT SUSPENSION:	Independent with coil spring struts
REAR SUSPENSION:	Independent with torsion bar
STEERING TYPE:	Power assisted rack-and-pinion
TURNING CIRCLE (CURB-TO-CURB):	33.8 feet
BRAKE TYPE:	Power-assisted front disc/rear disc
TIRE TYPE AND SIZE:	Front: P205/55R16; Rear: P225/50R16
WHEELBASE:	94.49 in.
LENGTH:	168.9 in.
WIDTH:	68.3 in.
HEIGHT:	50.2 in.
CURB WEIGHT:	2,866 pounds
TRUNK CARGO VOLUME:	10.4-cubic feet, plus 7.9-cubic feet (rear seat folded)
ACCELERATION, 0-60 MPH:	7.7 seconds
FUEL CONSUMPTION:	19-26 miles per gallon

BEST SPORTS CAR
Price Range: Under $20,000

Twenty thousand dollars puts you in the upper echelons of the sports car world. The difference from this category and the under $15,000 mark is more luxury features and the very latest in technology.

THE CONTENDERS*	WHOLESALE	RETAIL
1989 Chevrolet Corvette	$16,700	$19,350
1990 Nissan 300ZX	$17,450	$19,950
1988 Porsche 944	$11,575	$13,375

*Prices of Contenders are base prices which may vary in range from those of the winning model.

The Winner

1990 NISSAN 300ZX

What does $20,000 get you in the used sports car market? If you spend it on a 1990 Nissan 300ZX it gets you a great state-of-the-art sports car that was designed from a clean sheet of paper. Nissan set its goal very high when designing the 300ZX. "We will build the best sports car in the world," said Tumio Yoshida, the 300ZX project director.

The contenders from Chevrolet and Porsche undoubtedly shared that goal when they were putting the Corvette and 944, respectively, on paper. And, for under $15,000, we like the 1987 Porsche 944S. But, if you can go a little higher in price, you can get the 1990 300ZX which tops its competitors, since it is at least a generation ahead of them. The Corvette in its basic form debuted in 1984 and the 944 in 1983. While both sportsters have had continued refinement, they can not match the clean sheet redesign of the 1990 300ZX.

With the redesigned 300ZX, which retailed for $27,300 in 1990, Nissan has come full circle with its "Z-cars." The original 240Z debuted in the fall of 1969 and was a landmark sports car — a six-cylinder coupe with 150 horsepower and a bargain base price of $3,526. The 240Z, often described as a Japanese Jaguar XKE, was an instant sales sensation.

However, through the years as the Z-car evolved it steadily grew in size, to appeal not just to the sports car set, but to the wider base of car buyers that wanted a more luxury-oriented model and even 2+2 seating.

By the time the third generation ZX was introduced in 1983, the 300ZX was closer to being a Japanese Thunderbird than a Japanese XKE. Sales of the bulky, luxury performance car continued strong, but Nissan realized that the 300ZX was the image car for the entire automaker and should represent the firm's finest advanced technology.

Nissan went for a more squat, aggressive look for its new Z. The wheelbase was lengthened to 96.5 inches from 91.3 inches and the overall length shortened from 170.3 inches to 169.5 inches. A reduction in height, increase in width and radical 60-degree headlight lens completed the new curvaceous look. The hatchback and glass T-tops were carried over from the previous model. Later, a straight coupe, with no T-tops, was made available.

The pleasing and fluid exterior also proved to be very aerodynamic. The 300ZX has a drag coefficient of 0.31, lower than the Porsche 944, 0.33; and the Corvette, 0.34. In a real confirmation of the sleek new curves and willing engine, the 300ZX is quicker than the Corvette from 60 mph to 100 mph and carries the advantage up to 140 mph. The 300ZX also passes a more real world aerodynamic test — at highway speed — as wind noise is practically nonexistent.

The two-seat 300ZX also is available in a 2+2 version that is built on a 5.1 inch longer wheelbase, but it will cost you another $500. The 2+2 is so well proportioned that it is difficult to tell from the standard model. The only real exterior tipoff is that the fuel filler door is located behind the left rear wheel opening. Like most sporty 2+2 models, the rear folding seats are for occasional use only, and are best for small children, luggage and packages.

A much refined version of the previous model's 3.0-liter, V-6 engine is used with the 300ZX. The main improvement is a 24-valve cylinder head that results in 222 horsepower — 17 more horsepower than the previous year's turbocharged model. With the new engine, the 300ZX is capable of 0-60 mph in 7.1 seconds and a top speed of 148 mph.

If that is not enough performance, the 300ZX Turbo, for another $3,000, pumps out 300 horsepower and rips the pavement with 0-60 mph clockings of 5.5 seconds and a governor-limited top speed of 155 mph.

Bringing the 300ZX down to speed are four-wheel, vented disc brakes and standard ABS anti-lock brakes.

A Cray Supercomputer was used to design the '90 300ZX's front and rear suspension. The key to making the suspension work was an extremely rigid platform that would not deflect and alter the suspension settings and action. The '90 300ZX unibody is 35 percent stiffer in bending mode and 20 percent stronger in the torsional mode than the '89 model.

Size, Comfort and Style

The size of the 300ZX is functional — plenty of room for two passengers and all their luggage. By extending the wheelbase to 96.5 inches from the previous model's 91.3 inches and slightly shortening the overall length, Nissan engineers increased the passenger compartment space. Further gains were made by moving the cabin forward in the design.

Creature comfort level is high with most luxury car features standard equipment. The long list includes air conditioning, AM/FM stereo with cassette, power windows, T-bar sunroof, power outside mirrors, cruise control and central locking.

The 300ZX is a silent cruiser with its velvet smooth V6 and its clean aerodynamic lines kicking up little wind noise. At 60 mph, the 300ZX is loafing at 2,600 rpm.

Passenger comfort is enhanced by the well-thought out interior and a suspension design that achieves high-cornering limits without resorting to a stiff and hard ride. The front and rear multi-link suspension can maintain road contact with relatively soft springs, shock absorbers, anti-roll bars and suspension bushings.

The short front and rear overhang provides excellent visibility over the sloping hood. The overall visibility is good, except for the rear three-quarter view, which is hampered by the wide C-pillar. However, the excellent electric sideview mirrors more than compensate.

With its clean lines and balanced proportions, the 300ZX looks much smaller than it is in reality. The smooth-flowing lines from the sloping front end to the curve of the rear quarter windows are clean and uncluttered. There are no tacked on spoilers, flares or scoops.

ENGINE AND DRIVETRAIN

While the '90 300ZX and the '89 model both are powered by 3.0-liter V-6 engines, the only things shared between the two powerplants are the cylinder bore and stroke.

The new engine is rated at 222 horsepower at 6,400 rpm and 198 foot-pounds of torque at 4,800 rpm. The high output is impressive, especially when you consider the '89 300ZX Turbo version produced 17 less horsepower.

The '90 base 300ZX engine inhales deeply not with a turbocharger, but with a four-valve cylinder head. The total 24 valves are driven by a pair of camshafts for each cylinder bank. The four-valve heads feature pent-roof combustion chambers with centrally located sparkplugs to improve combustion efficiency.

The deep-breathing heads work in concert with a specially tuned induction system, a distributorless ignition system and variable valve timing.

The induction system, with multi-port fuel injection, uses long intake ram tubes to enhance low- and mid-range power. In addition, Nissan engineers tailored the intake tubes with an internal "aerodynamic port" that further increases the air velocity to pick up the bottom-end power.

Nissan's Direct Ignition System eliminates the conventional distributor, high-tension sparkplug wires and ignition coil. In place of the conventional units are a compact coil connected directly to each sparkplug. A crankshaft-mounted sensor and a computer engine management control unit triggers the spark to each cylinder.

The engine performance is further enhanced by a new variable valve timing system that changes the intake-valve timing. With conventional systems, the intake valves open and close in a compromise setting between optimum low- and high-speed running. The Nissan system, allows optimum timing throughout the rpm range, by varying the intake valve timing. The intake valves open and close sooner at lower speed and remain open longer at high speeds. The result is better low-end performance without any sacrifice in high-speed power.

If 222 horsepower is not enough motivation, the Nissan 300ZX Turbo generates 300 horsepower from a pair of turbochargers and matching intercoolers. For an additional $3,000, the Turbo is approximately 1.5 seconds quicker than the normally aspirated model in the 0-60 mph sprint.

HANDLING

The 300ZX has all the right ingredients needed for world class handling — beefy 16-inch tires, sophisticated multi-link suspension, viscous limited-slip differential, anti-lock brakes and responsive, variable-assist rack-and-pinion steering. The bottom line is the 300ZX just flat out works.

At the West Coast premier of the 300ZX at the famed Laguna Seca Raceway, the new Nissan proved it had what it takes when it comes to handling. The Monterey track's Turn Seven — an intimidating turn that is downhill, with a decreasing radius and off-camber — is a true test of great handling.

With a front-wheel-drive car, or a front-heavy conventional model at speed, Turn Seven induces mass quantities of understeer. You steer toward the turn, but instead the car wants to push the front tires straight off the intended path.

With a rear-engine car, or one with rear-weight bias, Turn Seven brings about oversteer — a condition where the rear tires attempt to come around and get better acquainted with the front.

Turn Seven can be tamed by choosing the right racing line and doing some fancy hand and foot work — Band-aid remedies for less than ideal suspensions and handling.

The 300ZX does not need any Band-aids when it comes to Turn Seven or any corner it tackles. Unlike lesser cars, the Nissan sports car maintains its poise and balance as it flat-out flies through the corner.

Balance and near neutral handling is what the 300ZX is about. There is just a trace of understeer that can be neutralized with application of the throttle. In moderation, this induced oversteer can help to rotate, or point the car, often the quickest way around a corner.

Brakes

The 300ZX brakes are very similar to units on true race cars. The four-wheel vented disc brakes feature opposed-piston calipers. Front calipers are a four-piston design, the rear use two pistons. The five-spoke alloy wheel is designed to show off the massive calipers and their Nissan logo.

The 16-inch wheels allow for huge 11.7-inch diameter front rotors and 11.0-inch rotors at the rear. The excellent braking system is topped off with an anti-lock braking system. The ABS prevents tire lockup and gives steering control under panic stops or slippery conditions. Stopping distance from 60 mph is 134 feet.

Ride Quality

Nissan was able to develop both ride comfort and excellent handling — often two mutually exclusive traits — because of its extremely solid unibody structure and sophisticated multi-link front and rear suspension that keeps the tires at optimum position without the need for stiff springs, overly firm shock absorbers and rigid anti-roll bar settings. The design also reduces distortion of the suspension's rubber bushings, so softer bushings can be used, further improving ride.

The ride is firm, but very well controlled. When cornering briskly over a rutted surface the rear suspension maintains its poise and smooths out the ride.

INTERIOR

The 300ZX interior is very driver oriented, with all the necessary controls right at hand. The top half of the leather-wrapped, three-spoke steering wheel frames the instrument panel that features a large analog tachometer and speedometer.

Dash-mounted modules on either side of the steering wheel house the controls — for heating, air conditioning, wipers, lights, cruise control and rear-window defogger — that are within easy reach from the steering wheel. The high center console defines the driver and passenger spaces.

The supportive seats are finished in a luxurious cloth interior that is carried out in the lower dash, console and door side panels. Standard creature comforts include air conditioning, AM/FM stereo with cassette, power windows, T-bar sunroof, power outside mirrors, cruise control and central locking. A premium Bose sound system is optional.

SUMMARY

The 1990 Nissan 300ZX tops its sports car rivals because it is the most modern and technological advanced offering. It is generations ahead of the Chevrolet Corvette, which debuted in 1984, and the Porsche 944, which was introduced in 1983.

It has nearly the acceleration of the Chevrolet Corvette and the handling of the Porsche 944, and its own kind of smoothness and refinement. It is not only a high-performance sports car, but also an effortless grand tourer.

Some may question if Nissan achieved its goal of building the best sports car in the world, but there is no doubt the 300ZX is the best used sports car for less than $20,000.

1990 NISSAN 300ZX

ASSETS
All-new, state-of-art design
Smooth V-6
Excellent handling

DEBITS
Limited engine access
Insurance surcharge

HOW THE RUNNERS-UP PLACED
FOLLOWING THE NISSAN 300ZX
2nd PLACE...The 1989 Chevrolet Corvette
Capable of impressive acceleration and handling numbers, but quality standards do not match competitors in this price range.
3rd PLACE...The Porsche 944
Good all-around performer, but 2.7-liter four-cylinder is not as smooth as the competition.

A CLOSER LOOK AT THE 1990 NISSAN 300ZX

SPECIFICATIONS:	Front engine, rear-wheel drive, two-door sports car with hatchback. Options include 2+2 and 300 horsepower, turbocharged version.
ENGINE:	V-6
DISPLACEMENT:	3.0 liter
HORSEPOWER:	222 @ 6,400 RPM
TORQUE:	198 foot-pounds @ 4,800 RPM
INDUCTION SYSTEM:	Multiport fuel injection
RECOMMENDED FUEL:	Unleaded premium

DRIVETRAIN:	Five-speed manual
FRONT SUSPENSION:	Independent multi-link with coil springs
REAR SUSPENSION:	Independent 5-link with coil springs
STEERING TYPE:	Power assisted, rack-and-pinion
TURNING CIRCLE (CURB-TO-CURB):	34.1 feet
BRAKE TYPE:	Power-assisted front disc/rear disc
TIRE TYPE AND SIZE:	P225/50VR16
WHEELBASE:	96.5 in.
LENGTH:	169.5in.
WIDTH:	70.5 in.
HEIGHT:	49.4 in.
CURB WEIGHT:	3,220 pounds
TRUNK CARGO VOLUME:	10-cubic feet
ACCELERATION, 0-60 MPH:	7.1 seconds
FUEL CONSUMPTION:	17-25 miles per gallon

BEST SPORTS CAR
Price Range: Over $20,000

The ideal sports car in this category has leading edge acceleration, handling and overall performance that is at home on a race track or cruising the boulevard. In addition, this high-performance ability comes wrapped in an eye-catching package that includes luxury creature comforts.

THE CONTENDERS*	WHOLESALE	RETAIL
1991 Acura NSX	$52,500	$57,500
1991 Chevrolet Corvette ZR-1 ...	$49,500	$53,500
1991 Porsche 911 Turbo	$66,000	$72,000

*Prices of Contenders are base prices which may vary in range from those of the winning model.

The Winner

1991 ACURA NSX

There are cars and then there are supercars. Used sports cars that cost more than $30,000 definitely have earned the right to wear an "S."

In addition to being very expensive, supercars have exotic looks, are produced in limited numbers, and boast of super performance levels that are best searched out on a race course.

However, there is a tradeoff with many supercars. They are uncomfortable, impractical for daily driving, have questionable reliability, and service and repairs are expensive and hard to find. These tradeoffs are true with many supercar marques such as Ferrari, Lamborghini and Lotus.

More practical alternatives have the supercar performance, but not the exotic styling and exclusivity. Supercars in this category include the Chevrolet Corvette and Porsche 911 series. Even in their most exotic forms — the Corvette ZR-1 and 911 Turbo — these cars do not standout like a true exotic.

The Acura NSX is alone when it comes to exclusivity, head-turning looks and everyday driveability. It has the look and performance of a Ferrari and the driveability and reliability of a Honda Accord.

The 1991 Acura NSX is the best sports car over $30,000 because it is the first, truly practical exotic car. The NSX is also a very elite car with just 3,000 being imported into the U.S. market annually.

Such exclusivity is very expensive. The suggested retail price of the NSX is $63,000 for the manual transmission version and $67,000 for the automatic model. When first introduced in the mid-1980's, the law of supply and demand shot the NSX price up to $100,000.

Now that enthusiasts who had to be first have been served, new NSX's are selling for suggested retail and slightly less. On the used car market, estimated current wholesale value is $52,500 and average retail $57,500.

Honda's work on the NSX began in 1984 with the goals matching or exceeding the performance of existing supercars, driveability, forgiving handling characteristics, limited production, and cockpit comfort on a par with its more standard Acura sedans and sports coupes.

To meet such lofty goals, Honda used technology from its Formula One engine that has powered McLaren to six straight Constructors' World Championships and five straight Drivers' World Championships. Many of the lessons learned on the race track found their way into the NSX.

The NSX is a two-seat, mid-engine sports car that is the world's first aluminum production car. Every major component is formed of aluminum for light weight to improve the car's power-to-weight ratio and handling. The use of aluminum for the entire body construction resulted in a 40 percent weight savings over an equivalent steel body. The complete body structure, including doors, hood and rear decklid, tips the scales at just 462 pounds.

Like the body-chassis, the suspension is made entirely of aluminum. The light weight suspension components reduce the car's unsprung weight and greatly improve handling.

A 3.0-liter, double-overhead cam, 24-valve V-6 engine powers the NSX. The potent powerplant's 270 horsepower can launch the NSX 0-60 miles per hour in just 5.03 seconds, according to Acura figures. Top speed is in excess of 160 mph.

Other outstanding innovations featured in the NSX include variable valve timing, variable volume induction system, traction control, titanium connecting rods, electronic power steering, four-channel anti-lock brakes, and a new airbag design.

The NSX is built in a dedicated plant in Tochigi, Japan — adjacent to Honda's research and development facility. Only 32 of the hand-built vehicles are produced per working day by the plant's 200 associates. The associates are hand-picked and each must have a minimum of 10 years of experience and distinguished past service.

Size, Comfort and Style

The aluminum-bodied NSX distributes its 3,010 pounds with 42 percent over the front tires and 58 percent over the rear tires of its 99.6-inch wheelbase. The front track is a wide 59.4 inches and the rear track is 60.2 inches. Overall length is 173.4 inches and the overall height is a low 46.1 inches.

Surprisingly, the NSX is about the same external size as a Corvette. The Chevrolet sports car is about five inches longer in length, two inches wider and about a half-inch taller than the NSX. Behind the steering wheel, the NSX seems much smaller than a Corvette as its sloping front end and 312 degrees of cockpit visibility give it an excellent view of the road and traffic.

The NSX was designed to provide the ultimate in comfort for two people.

The contoured bucket seats have excellent support and feature power adjustments. Creature comforts include leather interior, automatic climate control, Acura/Bose music system with four speakers and optional CD player, power windows and door locks, cruise control, and tilt and telescopic steering column.

The NSX has a "cab-forward" design that places the passenger compartment, or cab, proportionally forward in the design. The cab-forward layout was required by the mid-engine format. Acura engineers said they used the F-16 fighter jet as inspiration for styling the NSX.

The design has some Ferrari styling cues and features retractable headlights and bold side intakes located just behind the doors. The aerodynamic NSX has a drag coefficient rating of 0.32. The design emphasis is on total aerodynamics — a balance of lift, drag and yaw forces. The long tail design and the integrated rear spoiler help stabilize the car.

ENGINE AND DRIVETRAIN

The NSX is powered by an all-aluminum, 3.0-liter, double overhead cam, 24-valve engine rated at 270 horsepower at 7,100 rpm when mated to a manual transmission and 252 horsepower at 6,600 rpm when matched with the optional automatic transmission. Torque rating is 210 foot-pounds at 5,300 rpm for either transmission.

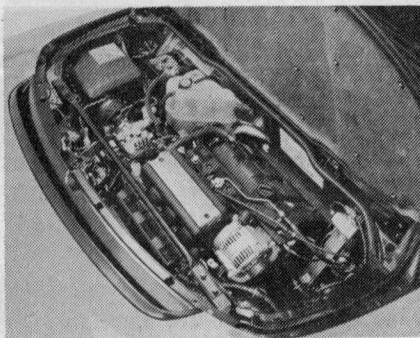

The engine has many innovations taken directly from Honda's experience with its dominating Formula One Grand Prix racing team. The NSX's titanium alloy connecting rods are the first application of titanium in a production car. The exotic material is common in Formula One race engines.

The NSX's electronic variable valve timing and variable volume intake system gives it good response at both low and high rpm ranges. The variable valve timing has three rocker arms and a special camshaft with three lobes. At low to middle speeds, two of the rockers work conventionally. As speeds climb to 5,800 rpm the third rocker locks together with the other two and the valve train is forced to follow the higher, more performance-oriented cam lobe.

The variable volume induction system is a two-stage system that opens up a secondary intake path between 4,600 and 4,900 rpm to boost intake volume and performance.

The standard transmission is a five-speed manual unit which transfers the NSX's power via a twin-disc clutch. The twin-disc design increases the torque capacity of the unit, while retaining a light clutch feel.

The optional automatic transmission allows the driver to select and hold each gear manually. To enhance smoothness during upshifts and downshifts, the engine ignition is retarded to momentarily reduce engine output. The automatic also comes with a variable electronic power-assist steering system that is not available on the manually transmissioned car.

HANDLING

Once again, Honda engineers drew on their Formula One experience to design the NSX suspension. The NSX has upper and lower control arms with a coil-over gas-pressurized shock absorber and anti-roll bars front and rear. The rear suspension has an additional transverse link for greater wheel control.

All suspension arms are made of extremely rigid and durable forged aluminum. The front steering knuckles and the rear hub carriers are also made from aluminum forgings.

With its biased wheel and tire sizes of P205/50ZR15 front and 225/50ZR16 rear, NSX has near neutral handling so that a skilled driver can induce oversteer with the throttle for all-out handling. The NSX has an extremely high lateral acceleration figure of 0.94 on the skid pad.

The steering is very precise and the car nearly impossible for any driver to lose control of, especially when the Traction Control System (TCS) is utilized. The TCS minimizes rear wheelspin on slippery or uneven road conditions by reducing engine power. Unlike most low-speed traction systems, TCS is a high-performance enhancement and can be disengaged by a switch on the instrument panel.

The suspension development was evaluated by racing drivers such as two-time Formula One World Champion Ayrton Senna and Indianapolis 500 winner Bobby Rahal.

Brakes

The NSX is equipped with four-wheel ventilated disc brakes and dual piston steel calipers. The diameter of the front and rear discs are 11.1 inches. The NSX has a four-channel anti-lock braking system. Anti-lock brakes prevent the tires from locking and losing traction no matter what the surface or condition and allows steering control to be maintained. The NSX stops from 60 miles per hour in just 128 feet.

Ride Quality

The ride quality is solid with firm control. The NSX does not have the soft ride of a luxury sedan, but its well-controlled ride is much better than the Corvette or the Porsche. The Porsche's suspension is stiffer than the NSX and the Corvette is even more firm. The NSX has an excellent touring and freeway ride.

INTERIOR

Seating position in the supportive bucket seats is low, but with the cab-forward design, the driver is positioned high in the 46.1-inch tall NSX.

The sloping hood and large greenhouse gives an excellent 312-degree view from the driver's seat.

The leather-covered steering wheel houses the driver's airbag and has controls for the cruise control. The steering wheel tilts and telescopes so nearly any driver can find the right position. The instrument panel has large white-on-black analog gauges that include speedometer, tachometer, temperature, fuel level, oil pressure and voltmeter.

Interior appointments include leather-trimmed power seats, automatic climate control, Acura/Bose music system, theft deterrent system and driver's side

airbag.

SUMMARY

Clearly, Acura has met its goal of producing a world class sports car. The NSX supercar has state-of-the-art innovations and designs straight from the race track and Honda's dominating Formula One racing team.

While as potent as a race car in acceleration, top speed and handling, the NSX can also be as docile as any Honda sedan. Unlike some exotic cars, with the NSX there is no fear of being unable to obtain proper service and parts. Acura has built its reputation on its quality-built vehicles and its dealerships' service to customers. Acura was ranked No. 1 in the J.D. Power and Associates "Customer Satisfaction Index" survey in 1987, '88, '89 and '90 — the first four years the automaker was eligible.

A used 1991 Acura NSX is priced much lower than the latest, unchanged new model and with its limited production should retain much of its value in the years to come.

1991 ACURA NSX

ASSETS	DEBITS
New state-of-the-art design	Limited interior storage
Tremendous performance	Small trunk
Driver's side airbag	
Anti-lock brakes	

HOW THE RUNNERS-UP PLACED
FOLLOWING THE ACURA NSX

2nd PLACE...1991 Porsche 911 Turbo

Tops the NSX performance, but at a much higher price and with a basic, less exotic design that originated in 1963 . NSX has superior ride.

3rd PLACE...1991 Chevrolet Corvette ZR-1

Potent LT-5 engine adds life to this generation of Corvette that debuted in the 1984 model year. NSX has less performance, but much more distinctive styling; ZR-1 does not look much different than a base L98 model. NSX has a far superior ride.

A CLOSER LOOK AT THE 1991 ACURA NSX

SPECIFICATIONS:	Mid-engine, two-wheel drive sports car with aluminum utilized body.
ENGINE:	V-6
DISPLACEMENT:	3.0 liter
HORSEPOWER:	270 @ 7,100 RPM
TORQUE:	210 foot-pounds @ 5,300 RPM
INDUCTION SYSTEM:	Electronic multiport fuel injection
RECOMMENDED FUEL:	Unleaded premium
DRIVETRAIN:	Five-speed manual
FRONT SUSPENSION:	Independent with upper and lower A-arms, coil springs, tube shocks, anti-roll bar
REAR SUSPENSION:	Independent with upper and lower A-arms, coil springs, tube shocks, anti-roll bar
STEERING TYPE:	Variable-ratio rack-and-pinion
TURNING CIRCLE (CURB-TO-CURB):	38.2 feet
BRAKE TYPE:	Power-assisted front and rear disc with anti-lock braking system
TIRE TYPE AND SIZE:	P205/50ZR15 front, P225/50ZR16 rear
WHEELBASE:	99.6 in.
LENGTH:	173.41 in.
WIDTH:	71.3 in.
HEIGHT:	46.1 in.
CURB WEIGHT:	3,010 pounds
TRUNK CARGO VOLUME:	5.4-cubic feet
ACCELERATION, 0-60 MPH:	5.03 seconds
FUEL CONSUMPTION:	19-24 miles per gallon

BEST MINIVAN

The key to selecting the best minivan, is its ability to comfortably move seven passengers and their luggage, while driving and handling like a car — not a truck.

THE CONTENDERS*	WHOLESALE	RETAIL
1990 Ford Aerostar Extended	$7,225	$8,400
1989 Mazda MPV	$7,700	$8,950
1990 Plymouth Grand Voyager SE	$10,000	$11,525

*Prices of Contenders are base prices which may vary in range from those of the winning model.

The Winner

1990 PLYMOUTH GRAND VOYAGER SE

What did we ever do before the minivan? It is hard to believe that these versatile people and cargo movers have only been around since 1984. Sure, short-wheelbase conventional vans and even the Volkswagen Microbus existed before, but they missed the mark.

The small, conventional vans performed exactly like what they were — smaller versions of full-size vans that drove and handled closer to a truck than a passenger car.

The VW Microbus, introduced in the U.S. in 1951, certainly was ahead of its time, but did not have the power and smoothness required for American driving. The 36-horsepower, 1.2-liter aircooled four-cylinder was inadequate for the U.S. masses.

Then in 1984, along comes an innovative breakthrough; a front-wheel-drive, people-mover that drove like a car and would fit inside the average garage. In addition, the design was bold and attractive and very fuel efficient.

The Chrysler minivans — twins Dodge Caravan and Plymouth Voyager — sold like hot cakes and soon were followed by minivans produced by nearly all the major automakers.

The minivan officially replaced the station wagon as the family hauler of choice. According to a Chrysler survey of its owners, 93 percent are married and nearly half have two or more children under age six.

Fast forward to 1992, and Chrysler, which has sold nearly 3 million minivans, is still leading the field. Chrysler has kept ahead of the minivan phenomenon by continuing to refine and improve its offerings.

In 1991, Chrysler increased its share of the minivan market from 41.1 percent to 45.0 percent. Its '91 sales total — including Caravan, Voyager and Chrysler Town & Country — of 395,119 units was up 14,745 units from the previous year and was achieved in a "down" market.

Part of the strong '91 percent can be attributed to Chrysler debuting its new generation of minivans with a host of improvements and options that include four-wheel drive, anti-lock braking system and driver's side airbag. In 1992, they faced increasing competition from improved rivals, especially the Mazda MPV.

As good as the '91 Chrysler minivans are, the '90 Plymouth Grand Voyager and its twin, the Dodge Grand Caravan, are the best used minivan because of their outstanding value. The '90 has many of the ongoing improvements and refinements of the '91, but costs thousands less on the used car market.

The '90 Grand Voyager has a current wholesale price of $10,000 and an average retail price of $11,525. The '91 however, has an estimated wholesale value of $12,650 and a retail value of $14,975.

If your situation requires the extra traction of four-wheel drive, the better control of anti-lock brakes and the security and safety of an airbag, shop for the '91 model. If these features are not that important to you, then buy a '90 and save about $4,000. The '90 will absolutely transport seven passengers and their luggage as well as the new model.

Some of the ongoing refinements made from 1984-90 include: electrically operated rear side vent windows, back seat control for the heating and cooling system, a pair of powerful optional V-6 engines, four-speed automatic transmission, a roomier, longer wheelbase version and added interior conveniences such as cupholders, map lights and coin holders.

Chrysler minivans are available in five trim levels — base, SE, LE and long-wheelbase Grand SE and Grand LE. The minivan can be outfitted to seat five or seven passengers. The five-passenger unit has a pair of front bucket seats and a rear three-passenger bench seat. The seven-passenger model adds a two-place center bench seat to the standard layout.

Four engines and three transmissions are available. There are a pair of four cylinder units and a pair of V-6 engines.

The Chrysler minivans have won numerous awards since being introduced in 1984. Public Broadcasting's popular Motorweek television show recently named the Chrysler Minivan "The Car of the Decade."

Size, Comfort and Style

The Voyager is available in two lengths; the standard and Grand model. The standard model has a 112-inch wheelbase and an overall length of 173 inches. The Grand version tapes out with a 119-inch wheelbase and an overall length of 190.5 inches. The Grand model is the best model as the additional 16.5 inches in length add an additional 25-cubic feet of interior volume. That translates into more leg room for passengers in the two bench seats and more cargo room behind the rear seat.

Even the Grand model is shorter than most full-size sedans. This makes the Voyager easy to handle and very maneuverable. In addition, the expansive glass area and the tall seating position give the driver an excellent view of the road and traffic all around.

The comfort level of the Voyager Grand is excellent, with roomy interior dimensions — 59.0 inches wide internally with a seating height of 48.0 inches — that allow passengers to slightly bend over and walk between the front seats to the rear section.

The engine and transaxle are well isolated and little, if any, mechanical noise reaches the interior. Flush glass and clean aerodynamics cut wind noise and contribute to the overall quiet cruising.

The styling of the Voyager is clean and straightforward. The extensive use of glass is effective in giving it a light and purposeful look. Compared to conventional vans, the lower height of the Voyager gives it a much more stable look.

The proportions are dictated by the placement of the transversally mounted engine, transaxle and driver's position. The powertrain is mounted ahead of the driver who sits behind the front axle centerline. The functional design gives plenty of access to the engine compartment.

The steeply sloping hood and aerodynamic details like flush-mounted side windows give the Voyager a drag coefficient of 0.42.

ENGINE AND DRIVETRAIN

The '90 Voyager is available with a choice of four engines. The base four-cylinder unit displaces 2.5-liter and is rated at 100 horsepower. The turbocharged version of the base engine pumps out 150 horsepower.

A Mitsubishi-built, 3.0-liter V-6 has a 142 horsepower output at 5,000 rpm and generates 173 foot-pounds of torque at 3,600 rpm. The Chrysler-built, 3.3-liter V-6 is good for 150 horsepower at 4,800 rpm and is rated at 185 foot-pounds of torque at 3,600 rpm.

The sixes are the only engines to consider when buying a Voyager. The base 2.5-liter engine is too small for the job and the turbo 2.5 develops its torque and horsepower too high in the rpm range. Chrysler brought out the turbo 2.5 to fill in for a shortage of -6s until the production of its own

3.3-liter unit got up to speed. The turbo 2.5 was dropped the following year.

Transmissions available were a five-speed manual, a three-speed automatic and the four-speed Ultradrive transmission. The manual unit feels out of place in a people mover like the Voyager and was dropped the following year. The three-speed automatic is a good choice and the Ultradrive has proven itself after a shaky start up and some running changes and updates.

A leading consumer magazine questioned the reliability of the Ultradrive unit, introduced in '89, which prompted Chrysler to personally telephone every owner of an Ultradrive-equipped car and see if they were satisfied. Chrysler, which did not charge even a warranty deductible for any needed updating of the early units, by now has repaired or replaced any defective units.

HANDLING

The Voyager drives and handles not like a conventional van or truck, but like a tall passenger car. The general attitude in hard cornering is typically front-wheel-drive understeer. The quality gives the Voyager good direction stability, even in cross winds.

Chrysler engineers have the front-wheel-drive platform tamed to not show negative traits such as torque steer and wheel hop. With its taller height, the Voyager displays more body roll than conventional sedans and the drive from the front wheels is invisible.

The front-wheel drive does show up in inclement weather when the road surface turns slick. With the majority of the minivan's weight over the front-driving wheels, traction is excellent and second only to four-wheel drive.

The front suspension features Chrysler's Iso-Strut design, lower A-arms, coil springs and gas-pressurized shock absorbers and an anti-roll bar. At the rear, the suspension has parallel leaf springs with a beam axle and gas-pressurized shock absorbers.

The steering mechanism is power-assisted and rack-and-pinion. Curb-to-curb turning diameter is 40.5 feet with the standard Voyager and 42.5 feet with the stretch Grand Voyager.

Brakes

Power-assisted front disc and rear drum brakes are standard on the Voyager. The front discs measure 10.2 inches in diameter and the rear drums have a diameter of 8.98 inches. From 60 miles per hour, the Grand Voyager stops in 166 feet. The larger optional P205/70R14 or P205/70R15 tires will further improve the overall braking performance from the standard P195/75R14 tires.

Ride Quality

The long 119-inch wheelbase of the Grand Voyager gives it a ride comparable to a sedan. However, ride quality is enhanced by the comfortable captain's-type seating of the front seat and roomy rear seat areas.

INTERIOR

Interior comfort and spaciousness is why you buy a minivan. The Grand Voyager with its additional 16.5 inches of length, and smooth operating sliding door, is the perfect people hauler for up to seven passengers.

Front seat passengers sit high in captain's-type bucket seats. The seats have comfortable armrests that can swing up out of the way when not in use. By swinging the armrest up, front seat passengers can easily move to the rear compartment. This is ideal for parents that want to check on their children in the back seats. The supportive front buckets recline and a six-way power driver's seat is available. The Voyager's glove compartment is located under the front passenger seat and is much roomier than a standard glove box.

With seven-passenger seating, the center bench seat holds two passengers and has swing up outside armrests. The rearmost seat holds three passengers and the seat back folds down so that the entire bench slides forward to allow more cargo space.

Other nice interior touches include an overhead console with individual map lights for the driver and front seat passenger, electrically operated flip-out rear windows and cupholders, small storage areas throughout the passenger compartment, and removable rear bench seats.

SUMMARY

The Chrysler minivans were the first of a new breed of family vehicles. Constant improvement and refinement resulted in the 1990 Plymouth Voyager Grand Voyager SE.

The V-6 engines give the Voyager good power and performance. The Voyager does not handle like a van, but it handles like a tall sedan, with an excellent commanding view of the roadway and traffic.

The stretch Grand model has extra room between the seating areas for improved leg room and has more cargo space. The rear bench seats can be individually removed for even more passenger-cargo flexibility.

The nation's minivan buyers are overwhelmingly voting for the Chrysler minivans, which accounted for 45 percent of the total minivan market in 1991.

The '90 Voyager has many of the features found in the rebodied '91 version, but is nearly $4,000 cheaper in the used car market. If you can get by without the '91's standard driver's airbag and optional anti-lock brakes and four-wheel drive, the '90 model is a much better value.

1990 PLYMOUTH GRAND VOYAGER SE

ASSETS	DEBITS
Car-like handling	Difficult to remove rear bench seats
Smooth V-6 engine	Limited towing capacity
Spacious interior	

HOW THE RUNNERS-UP PLACED
FOLLOWING THE PLYMOUTH GRAND VOYAGER SE
2nd PLACE... 1989 Mazda MPV

Rear-wheel drive makes it better than the Voyager in towing situations.

The 1989 can not match the ride and people-load capacity of the 8.6-inch longer wheelbase of the Voyager.

3rd PLACE... 1990 Ford Aerostar Extended

Extended version can match the stretch Voyager in interior space, but is not as car-like in ride and handling as the Voyager.

A CLOSER LOOK AT THE 1990 PLYMOUTH GRAND VOYAGER

SPECIFICATIONS:	Front engine, front-wheel drive, minivan.
ENGINE:	V-6
DISPLACEMENT:	3.0 liter
HORSEPOWER:	142 @ 5,000 RPM
TORQUE:	173 foot-pounds @ 3,600 RPM
INDUCTION SYSTEM:	Electronic multiport fuel injection
RECOMMENDED FUEL:	Unleaded regular
DRIVETRAIN:	Four-speed automatic
FRONT SUSPENSION:	Independent Iso-Strut, with coil springs, gas-pressurized shock absorbers and anti-roll bar
REAR SUSPENSION:	Parallel leaf spring with beam axle, gas-pressurized shock absorbers
STEERING TYPE:	Power assisted rack-and-pinion
TURNING CIRCLE (CURB-TO-CURB):	42.5 feet
BRAKE TYPE:	Power-assisted front disc/rear drum
TIRE TYPE AND SIZE:	P205/70R15
WHEELBASE:	119.0 in.
LENGTH:	190.5 in.
WIDTH:	72.0 in.
HEIGHT:	64.5 in.
CURB WEIGHT:	4,129 pounds
TRUNK CARGO VOLUME:	98.5-cubic feet with center and rear bench seats removed
ACCELERATION, 0-60 MPH:	12 seconds
FUEL CONSUMPTION:	19-24 miles per gallon

BEST FULL-SIZE VAN

The premium here is the ability to achieve comfort, handling and ride for up to 15 passengers.

THE CONTENDERS*	WHOLESALE	RETAIL
1990 Chevrolet Sportsvan	$8,900	$10,275
1990 Dodge B150 Wagon	$8,975	$10,375
1990 Ford Club Wagon	$9,975	$11,500

*Prices of Contenders are base prices which may vary in range from those of the winning model.

The Winner

1990 CHEVROLET SPORTSVAN

While full-size vans have taken a back seat to the popular minivans since 1984, there are times when there is no substitute for a big van. The Chevrolet Sportsvan, with its wide variety of options and features tops the field when it comes to customizing a unit for work or play.

Minivans are the top sellers, but there are many situations where even an extended-length minivan is not up to the task. Need to transport 15 passengers? The solution is either one full-size van, or a pair of minivans. What makes more sense?

Want to be able to tow a boat or a trailer weighing more than 6,000 pounds? The only way is with the low-end grunt and power of a V-8 engine — not found in any minivan, but common in a full-size van.

If you are a diesel fan, you can forget about minivans, but diesels are options on full-size vans. If you have a large family, an extended-wheelbase, full-size van with seating for 15 is the ticket.

While the big V-8s in maxivans won't win any fuel economy contests, the actual cost per passenger is impressive when compared with two 20 miles per gallon minivans needed to match their passenger and towing capacity.

The Chevrolet Sportsvan and its GMC Rally/Vandura twin get the nod over the competition because of a new for '90 extended model and the widest range of powerplants — from V-6s to V-8s, a pair of diesels and a monster 7.4-liter V-8.

The extended version is available in the G30 series Sportsvan and features the 5.7-liter V-8 with electronic fuel injection. The engine is mated with a heavy-duty three-speed automatic and a 3.73-to-1 final drive ratio. The package carries a 8,600-pound Gross Vehicle Weight Rating. The wheelbase is 146 inches, up from 125 inches of the base model. The overall length is up 21 inches to 223.2.

The extended Sportsvan is available in standard or premium Beauville trim. The platform is outfitted for 12 passengers with generous room behind the seat for cargo. An optional bench seat increases the capacity to 15 passengers. The Beauville option adds about $2,900 to the 1992 retail value.

New standard trim in '90 includes heavy-duty power brakes, anti-lock rear brakes, tinted glass on all windows, swing-out rear door glass, intermittent wipers, side-window defoggers, electronically tuned AM radio, heavy-duty battery, halogen headlamps, chromed bumpers front and rear, 33-gallon fuel tank, full-length headliner and positive rear-door stop.

If you are interested in hauling cargo and not people, the Sportsvan is also available in a commercial counterpart, the Chevyvan. The Chevyvan is also available in an extended series model. Cargo volume is 306 cubic feet and the load floor length is 12.3 feet.

The base Chevyvan is truly a working model, with only a driver's high-back front bucket seat standard. The cargo van is targeted to a wide audience that includes commercial plumbers, carpet installers, ambulance and recreational conversion markets. The Chevyvan also is perfect for carrying weekend toys like jet skis and motorcycles.

The recreational vehicle industry is very interested in the Chevrolet Sportsvan platform. The conversions by private contractors range from mild to wild.

A mild facelift by a converter might include a more plush interior with four swiveling, high-back captains chairs with armrests. From there additions could include an ice box, sink, premium sound system, special lighting, window shades and thick carpeting.

The converters also tackle the exterior with front air dams, rear spoilers, very functional running boards, and flared fenders to cover wide alloy wheels and low-profile tires.

A full-blown recreational van conversion is fully self-contained. The conversion can include a specially fitted, raised roof section that allows standing room, a propane/electric oven and stove, microwave, hot and cold running water, bathroom and shower.

A converted mini-motor home van is a rolling example of space efficiency. While such a conversion will boast the comforts of home, it still is small enough to serve double duty and be driven everyday.

Size, Comfort and Style

The size and maneuverability of a Sportsvan or Chevyvan is directly dependent on the wheelbase of the platform. The 110-inch wheelbase model definitely has the shortest turning circle and is easier to maneuver with its

178.2-inch length.

Next in line is the 125-inch model with its 202.2-inch overall length. The extended model has a 146-inch wheelbase and stretches out to a total length of 223.2 inches.

While the maneuverability goes down with the longer platforms, the comfort and interior room is greatly enhanced. The longer versions are ideal for the magic performed by van conversion firms. There is plenty of room to place swiveling captain's chairs and a table to hold drinks and even lunch. The comfort potential for a Sportsvan is only limited by the owner's imagination and budget.

The Sportsvan's exterior style can range from plain Jane to bold and flashy. In addition to the exterior add ons — spoilers, flares, running boards etc...— the large expanses of body panels are perfect for a mural. The sky is the limit.

ENGINE AND DRIVETRAIN

The heart of the Chevrolet full-size van is its wide-ranging lineup of powerplants which includes the venerable Chevrolet small-block V-8.

The standard engine is the 4.3-liter, Vortec V-6 with roller valve lifters for reduced friction. This rugged V-6 is based on the famous small-block V-8 and shares the same pistons, rods and many other parts with the 5.7-liter V-8. The electronic fuel-injected V-6 is rated 150 horsepower at 4,000 rpm

Five optional V-8 engines are available — 5.0-liter, 5.7-liter and 7.4-liter units burning gasoline, and a pair of 6.2-liter diesels. All gasoline engines feature computer-controlled, throttle-body fuel injection for precise fuel control and fuel economy.

An automatic is standard on all models. The availability of a four-speed automatic with overdrive or a heavy-duty three-speed automatic depends on the model.

The small-block Chevrolet V-8 has a well-earned reputation for reliability. It is not uncommon for owners to roll up 200,000 trouble-free miles with only oil and filter changes every 3,000 miles.

The 5.0-liter V-8 pumps out 170 horsepower at 4,000 rpm and 255 foot-pounds of torque at 2,400 rpm.

One of the most popular engine/transmission combinations is the 5.7-liter V-8 teamed with the four-speed automatic transmission. The 5.7 is rated at

190 horsepower at 4,000 rpm with 300 foot-pounds of torque at 2,400 rpm. The package provides excellent overall performance, from running downtown to towing a boat, expect about 16 to 18 miles per gallon.

For real serious towing and hauling, look for a Sportsvan equipped with the 7.4-liter V-8 that is rated at 230 horsepower. The big V-8 is the most powerful engine available in a Chevrolet light-duty truck. It boasts electronic spark control to regulate the spark advance and control knock.

The 7.4-liter unit is part of the Chevrolet heritage of big-block "rat" engines. The big Chevrolet engine has proven itself and is famous in race circles in 396- and 427-cubic inch variations.

Van buyers looking for a little more economy, can opt for the V-6. The V-6 when teamed with a four-speed automatic is rated at 16 miles per gallon city and 21 highway.

Diesel buyers can choose between a pair of diesel units. Both powerplants displace 6.2-liters, but differ in horsepower and torque. The standard diesel is rated at 145 horsepower at 3,600 rpm and 255 foot-pounds of torque at a low 1,900 rpm. The heavy-duty diesel churns out 155 horsepower at 3,600 rpm and 270 foot-pounds of torque at 2,000 rpm.

Any of the engine combinations offer excellent underhood accessibility.

Ford nearly matches Chevrolet in available powerplants, but Chevrolet gets the nod because its Votec V-6 is a more sophisticated unit than the inline Ford six. The Dodge van lacks a diesel option and its largest 5.9-liter V-8 falls short of both Chevrolet and Ford.

HANDLING

The Sportsvan exhibits solid and predictable handling. The independent coil-spring front suspension is anchored by a huge 1.06-inch front stabilizer bar to reduce sway.

Power steering is standard on all models and is definitely needed. The Sportsvan is definitely not a race car when it comes to handling. It's more suited for towing your race car. However, it has very predictable handling. Also predictable is the understeer, or front-end plow, with the front-heavy van.

When driving a Sportsvan, or any full-size van, it is best to look ahead and prepare to make your lane changes, turns and other maneuvers. This "big picture" technique of driving is very easy to do with the Sportsvan as its high-seating perch gives an excellent view of the road ahead. With the Sportsvan you do not have to try to look through cars ahead and behind you, you look over them.

Brakes

Power front disc and rear drum brakes are standard on all models. A rear-wheel anti-lock braking system is also standard on all models. The ABS system is designed to reduce rear-wheel lock-up during severe braking applications regardless of weight differences over the rear axle. Using a control valve located between the master cylinder and the rear brakes, the ABS system modulates rear brake line pressure and enables the driver to maintain critical steering control during severe braking.

Ride Quality

Ride quality is excellent, particularly with the upgraded Beauville trim level and the extended wheelbase. The long 146-inch wheelbase dampens bumps and smooths out all motions.

The improved insulation of the Beauville level also reduces road noise and vibration. Like most full-size vans, the Sportsvan has a smoother highway ride when the unit is loaded to its weight capacity.

INTERIOR

The Sportsvan is more like a small bus than a large passenger car. There is room in every direction to stretch out. There is also enough headroom to get up while underway and easily change seats and views.

Like General Motors' passenger cars, the Sportsvan is blessed with GM's outstanding heating and cooling system.

The instrument grouping consists of a high-tech cluster of round gauges. The speedometer is electrically driven for more accuracy.

The interior layout ranges from two vinyl bucket seats with the Chevyvan, to plush cloth buckets and three rows of bench seats for a seating capacity of 15 passengers. With a van conversion, a popular seating arrangement is four swiveling captain's chairs.

SUMMARY

Chevrolet's Sportsvan tops its Dodge B150 Wagon and Ford Club Wagon rivals with its new extended wheelbase option and a solid selection of powerplants. The Beauville trim level also brings it up to the luxury car level. The Sportsvan is very popular with the van conversion industry and many dealerships sell more conversions than standard vans. A used van conversion can be an excellent buy, as with depreciation, the original buyer ultimately pays for the majority of the conversion costs.

1990 CHEVROLET SPORTSVAN

ASSETS	DEBITS
Roomy interior	Large turning circle
Anti-lock rear brakes	
Proven powerplants	
Extended wheelbase option	

HOW THE RUNNERS-UP PLACED
FOLLOWING THE CHEVROLET SPORTSVAN

2nd PLACE...The Ford Club Wagon

A proven van that was overdue for its 1992 reskinning. Base inline six is outdated compared to Chevy's V-6 or V-8.

3rd PLACE...The Dodge D100

Reliable, but limited engine options, no diesel model available.

A CLOSER LOOK AT THE 1990 CHEVROLET SPORTSVAN

SPECIFICATIONS:	Front engine, rear-wheel drive, van. Options include 110-, 125- and 146-inch wheelbase versions.
ENGINE:	V-8 gasoline
DISPLACEMENT:	5.7 liter

HORSEPOWER:	190 @ 4,000 RPM
TORQUE:	300 foot-pounds @ 2,400 RPM
INDUCTION SYSTEM:	Electronic fuel injection
RECOMMENDED FUEL:	Unleaded regular
DRIVETRAIN:	Three-speed automatic
FRONT SUSPENSION:	Independent with coil springs
REAR SUSPENSION:	Multi-leaf rear springs
STEERING TYPE:	Variable-ratio, power assisted
TURNING CIRCLE (CURB-TO-CURB):	49 feet
BRAKE TYPE:	Power-assisted front disc/rear drum
TIRE TYPE AND SIZE:	P205/75R15
WHEELBASE:	125 in.
LENGTH:	178.2 in.
WIDTH:	79.5 in.
HEIGHT:	79.5 in.
CURB WEIGHT:	3,698 pounds
TRUNK CARGO VOLUME:	306 cubic feet
ACCELERATION, 0-60 MPH:	Approximately 10 seconds
FUEL CONSUMPTION:	Approximately 16-18 miles per gallon

BEST COMPACT SPORT UTILITY VEHICLE
Price Range Under $16,000

A compact sport utility vehicle has four-wheel drive and can carry up to five passengers and their cargo. The best have four doors along with power and good manners on- and off-road.

THE CONTENDERS*	WHOLESALE	RETAIL
1989 Nissan Pathfinder SE Sport .	$11,875	$13,725
1988 Jeep Cherokee Limited	$10,550	$12,100
1990 Toyota 4Runner SR5 V6 ...	$13,400	$15,725

*Prices of Contenders are base prices which may vary in range from those of the winning model.

The Winner

1990 TOYOTA 4RUNNER SR5

The utility and off-road capabilities of a four-wheel-drive truck combined with the ride and comfort of a five-passenger car, is the definition of a sport utility vehicle. Add one more item — four doors.

In the current market, four-doors for no waiting passenger ingress and egress has nearly become mandatory. With a compact sport utility, getting to the back seat in a two door requires a lot of climbing, twisting and bending. It has been compared to inviting someone over to your house and then asking them to climb through a window to come inside.

Before 1984, there were no production sport utility vehicles with four doors. Jeep introduced its Cherokee-Wagoneer in the '84 model year. From the beginning both were engineered with two and four doors.

Initial sales confirmed Jeep's marketing projections that the public wanted a four-door vehicle with the safety and security of four-wheel drive. The four-door model far outsells the two-door.

More significantly, the new Jeeps pioneered the sport utility vehicle's acceptance as an upscale alternative to a conventional car. The ultimate yuppie vehicle in California went from a BMW to a Jeep Cherokee Limited.

While four-door Jeep sales took off, rival automakers rushed to the drawing boards to develop their own four-door sport utility vehicles.

Jeep was joined by the Isuzu Trooper II in '87 and the Mitsubishi Montero in '89. It was not until the '90 model year that Toyota and Nissan brought out their four-door 4Runner and Pathfinder, respectively.

However, for the Toyota 4Runner, it was worth the wait. The '90 version is an all-new model that included four doors along with a long list of improvements and refinements, making it the best used compact sport utility vehicle under $16,000.

The original 4Runner was nothing more than a slightly modified pickup with a tacked on fiberglass shell and a rear bench seat. The '90 4Runner is a legitimate wagon with the interior comfort of a passenger sedan and all new sheetmetal.

The 4Runner is available in four versions: a two-wheel-drive, four-door SR5 V6; two-door, four-wheel-drive SR5 V6; four-door, four-wheel-drive SR5 with a 2.4-liter four-cylinder engine; and the four-door, four-wheel-drive SR5 V6.

The later model is the best of the 4Runner lineup and includes the 3.0-liter, 150-horsepower V-6, four-wheel-drive and the choice of a five-speed manual transmission or a four-speed automatic with overdrive.

For off-road treks, the 4Runner is protected with chip-resistant paint, plastic chip guards attached to the front and rear wheel wells and resin wheel arch liners. In addition, there are durable steel skid plates protecting the fuel tank, transfer case and front suspension.

Standard comfort features include full door trim with armrests, tinted glass, power rear window with wiper, driver-side foot rest, one-touch door locks, day-night rearview mirror and locking glove box.

With the split rear seat folded forward, the 4Runner's cargo volume grows from 43.5-cubic feet to 78.6-cubic feet. An optional luggage rack increases luggage capacity even more for long trips. Other options include a power sliding sunroof with sunshade, running boards, cold weather kit, aluminum wheels, deluxe electronically tuned stereo with cassette and four speakers and a stereo with CD system.

All 4Runners come standard with Toyota's legendary reliability. Since the 4Runner is very similar to the Toyota pickup from the firewall forward and shares the same powertrain, it is as rugged and reliable.

The '90 4Runner took top honors as the best compact sport utility vehicle in the J.D. Power and Associates Compact Truck Customer Satisfaction Index. The 4Runner was also the first compact sport utility vehicle to ever break the 100-problems-per-100-vehicle barrier in the J.D. Power 1991 New Compact Truck Initial Quality Study.

Size, Comfort and Style

The 4Runner's 4,145 pounds are carried over a 103.3-inch wheelbase and an overall length of 176.0 inches. The 4Runner looks much bigger than it really is because of the high 9.1-inch ground clearance Toyota built in the vehicle. This gives the 4Runner a macho look of being a serious off-road device and ready to take on the Baja 500.

However, the tradeoff is a high step up to the interior. The optional running boards are good choices, as they reduce the height of that first step.

Once inside the cab, the interior accommodations and comfort are on line with a passenger car. The 4Runner can also be outfitted as well as a luxury car. The driving position is good and the seats supportive. The rear bench has room for three passengers and is comfortable for two.

What really makes the 4Runner a comfortable vehicle is its silence. Toyota has managed to make the 4Runner as quiet at highway speeds as its sedans and quieter than many other sedans.

The new curved, aerodynamic styling contributes to the quiet ride by generating very little wind noise. The overall styling is big and bold with the high-ground clearance and the 4Runner body sitting above its aggressive P225/75R15 tires, even larger 31x10.5 tires are available. Unlike the previous model, the 4Runner's body is well integrated and is highlighted by flared fenders at each corner and large glass areas that, along with the high commanding view, give it excellent visibility from the driver's seat.

ENGINE AND DRIVETRAIN

The base engine is a 2.4-liter, electronically fuel injected, four-cylinder engine that produces 116 horsepower at 4,800 rpm and 140 foot-pounds of torque at 2,800 rpm.

The SR5 V6 offers the additional power and smoothness of a 3.0-liter, 150-horsepower V-6 engine that generates 150 horsepower at 4,800 rpm and 180 foot-pounds of torque at 3,400 rpm.

The 4Runner comes standard with a five-speed manual transmission or an optional 4-speed electronically controlled automatic transmission (ECT). At the touch of a button, the ECT offers the driver either a normal setting for fuel economy or a performance setting for enhanced acceleration.

The manual unit has a final drive ratio of 4.30:1, or 4.56:1 when the taller optional 31x10.5 tires are in order. The automatic's final drive ratio is 4.56:1, or 4.87:1 with the 31x10.5 tires.

The 4Runner does not offer pushbutton ease to shift into four-wheel drive like the Ford Explorer, but the center console-mounted transfer case lever is easy to operate and smoothly shifts from two-wheel to four-wheel-drive and back again. The unit allows shifting into four-wheel drive — even four-wheel-drive low range — while moving slowly.

The powerplant is smooth and response and power are fine for everyday driving. However, in off-road treks and when fully loaded or pulling a trailer, the 4Runner could benefit from more horsepower.

EPA-rated fuel economy of the automatic 4Runner SR5 V6 is 15 miles per gallon city and 19 mpg highway. Maximum trailer-towing capacity is 3,500 pounds.

HANDLING

Handling is safe and predictable with understeer and body lean when taking tight corners. The body roll is partly due to the high ground clearance for four-wheel drive and raised body of the 4Runner.

The front suspension is independent with torsion bar springing, upper and lower A-arms, gas-pressurized shock absorbers and an anti-roll bar. The rear suspension features a four-link live axle with coil springs and anti-roll bar.

When compared to compact 4x4 competitors with less sophisticated suspensions and a live front axle, the Toyota has a definite edge.

Caution should be noted when driving any four-wheel-drive sport utility vehicle. The inherent high ground clearance and high center of gravity in abrupt handling maneuvers results in a great deal of body roll. All sport utility vehicles, no matter the make, should not be driven like a sports car.

Brakes

Power front ventilated disc and rear drum brakes are standard on all models. A rear-wheel anti-lock braking system is also standard on all models. The ABS system is designed to reduce rear-wheel lock-up during severe braking applications regardless of weight differences over the rear axle. From 60 miles per hour, the 4Runner stops in 145 feet.

Ride Quality

On most roads and definitely on freeways, the 4Runner surprisingly has the ride quality and silence of a passenger car. The 4Runner's independent front suspension with its gas-pressurized shock absorbers gives it an excellent ride relative to other sport utility vehicles.

On back roads and off-road, the 4Runner's suspension bias toward paved freeways begins to show up as the relatively soft suspension is pushed to its limits. If you plan to do much rough- or off-road work, invest in a host of available aftermarket suspension components.

INTERIOR

The 4Runner interior is designed to be very passenger-car like and even luxurious if the right options are selected.

The form-fitting, cloth-covered front bucket seats are supportive and are outfitted with head restraints. The door panels are covered in matching cloth material.

The instrument panel is clearly laid out and easy to read. The two main gauges — speedometer and tachometer are mounted in the center portion of the instrument cluster and are flanked by gauges for water temperature, oil pressure, battery voltage and fuel level.

The transmission shift and four-wheel-drive transfer case lever are located on the central console along with the two-mode power switch for the ECT automatic transmission.

The rear seat can hold three 6-foot adults, but is much more comfortable for two passengers. The bottom cushion tumbles forward and the split seat backs fold down flush with the cargo area. The rear seats can be folded down independently when mixing cargo and passengers. When both seat backs are folded down, cargo space jumps from 43.5-cubic feet to 78.6-cubic feet.

Interior options include cruise control, seven-way adjustable sport seats, a large power sunroof, tuned speakers, CD stereo system, and various upgraded AM/FM stereo radios with cassette systems.

SUMMARY

The 1990 Toyota 4Runner SR5 V6 is an excellent used car buy and outdistances many of its competitors with its fresh, all-new design. It is no longer a pickup with a camper shell. Toyota has done a good job in combining the off-road capabilities of a truck with the creature comforts and ride of a passenger car.

Toyota 4Runner owners are also sold on the vehicle, because it took top honors as the best compact sport utility vehicle in the J.D. Power and Associates Compact Truck Customer Satisfaction Index.

A 4Runner is a Toyota and shares the Japanese automaker's reputation for quality fit and finish and mechanical durability and reliability.

1990 TOYOTA 4RUNNER SR5

ASSETS	DEBITS
All-new design for 1990	Could use more horsepower
Anti-lock rear brakes	High fuel consumption
Ranked No. 1 in customer satisfaction	

HOW THE RUNNERS-UP PLACED
FOLLOWING THE TOYOTA 4RUNNER SR5

2nd PLACE... 1989 Nissan Pathfinder SE Sport

Excellent ride, but passenger comfort and cargo space is less than the 4Runner.

3rd PLACE... 1988 Jeep Cherokee Limited

A sport utility pioneer in 1984 that is reaching the end of its design cycle. The 1993 Grand Cherokee is a big improvement.

A CLOSER LOOK AT THE 1990 TOYOTA 4RUNNER SR5

SPECIFICATIONS:	Front engine, four-wheel drive, four-door sport utility vehicle
ENGINE:	V-6

DISPLACEMENT:	3.0 liter
HORSEPOWER:	150 @ 4,800 RPM
TORQUE:	180 foot-pounds @ 3,400 RPM
INDUCTION SYSTEM:	Electronic multiport fuel injection
RECOMMENDED FUEL:	Unleaded regular
DRIVETRAIN:	Four-speed automatic
FRONT SUSPENSION:	Independent torsion bar with anti-roll bar
REAR SUSPENSION:	Four-link coil spring with anti-roll bar
STEERING TYPE:	Power assisted recirculating ball
TURNING CIRCLE (CURB-TO-CURB):	37.4 feet
BRAKE TYPE:	Power-assisted front disc/rear drum
TIRE TYPE AND SIZE:	P225/75R15
WHEELBASE:	103.3 in.
LENGTH:	176.0 in.
WIDTH:	66.5 in.
HEIGHT:	66.1 in.
CURB WEIGHT:	4,145 pounds
TRUNK CARGO VOLUME:	43.5-cubic feet, 78.6-cubic feet with rear seat folded down
ACCELERATION, 0-60 MPH:	12 seconds
FUEL CONSUMPTION:	15-19 miles per gallon

BEST FULL SIZE SPORT UTILITY VEHICLE

The ideal full-size sport utility vehicle, with a minimum wheelbase of 110 inches, must be rugged enough for four-wheel driving in the hills on the weekends and domesticated enough to handle carpooling the kids during the week.

THE CONTENDERS*	WHOLESALE	RETAIL
1991 Chevrolet Suburban	$13,975	$16,350
1991 Ford Explorer XL	$13,625	$16,000
1991 Toyota Landcruiser	$19,250	$22,300

*Prices of Contenders are base prices which may vary in range from those of the winning model.

The Winner

1991 FORD EXPLORER XL

The contemporary, full-size sport utility vehicle is a space vehicle. Ideally, it must have plenty of interior space for six passengers and all their camping equipment for a weekend outing, for a carpool full of children on weekday treks to school, for 50-pound bags of dog food, groceries and the occasional piece of furniture.

Of course, the ideal sport utility vehicle must also have four-wheel-drive for the rare off-road detour and added traction in inclement weather. It must be comfortable and practical enough to serve as an everyday passenger car.

The Ford Explorer does all the above and even more, making it the No.1 choice in used full-size sport utility vehicles. *Four Wheeler* magazine also concurs, having named it "Four Wheeler of the Year" in 1990 and again in 1991.

The buying public also voted for the Explorer. Introduced in March 1990 as a 1991 model, the Explorer quickly rose to the top in sales in the competitive sport utility vehicle market. It has never relinquished that front-running position.

The Explorer represents one of the most successful new-vehicle introductions in the North American light truck market. Explorer sales account for nearly 31 percent of the sales in its market segment.

The Explorer sales include many buyers that have crossed over from the automobile market. The Explorer is a viable alternative because of its unique blend of versatility, truck toughness, "car-like" comforts and conveniences, exceptional roominess and attractive, contemporary styling.

Ford engineers started with a clean sheet of paper when they began designing the replacement for the Bronco II. A high priority was space for passengers and cargo. The Explorer can seat five passengers with its standard front buckets seats and split-folding rear bench seat. An optional split bench front seat in XL and XLT models brings the passenger load up to six.

When the rear seat is up, objects up to 38.1 inches can be fitted into the generous storage area behind the rear seat. By folding the rear seat down, objects up to 72.9 inches can be handled. The Cargo volume with the rear seat up is 42.6-cubic feet and nearly doubles to 81.6-cubic feet when the rear seat is down.

Access to the cargo area is excellent and well thought out. The entire rear liftgate can be raised, or the window alone can be independently opened. Very convenient depending on the cargo you are carrying.

Explorers are available in six variations and with two-wheel or four-wheel drive. Trim levels for the two-door models are XL, Sport and Eddie Bauer. The four-door Explorer is available in XL, XLT and Eddie Bauer, the most expensive. The higher-line XL and XLT models have standard equipment that includes air conditioning, a power equipment group that includes power windows, door locks, electric remote-control mirrors; premium electronic AM/FM stereo with cassette, rear window wiper and defroster, tinted privacy glass, cargo cover, special light group, steering-wheel mounted cruise control and alloy wheels.

The Eddie Bauer package, named after the famous outdoor outfitter catalog store, adds a luggage rack, larger P235/70R15 all-terrain tires, sport bucket seats with leather seating surfaces, a center console, and Eddie Bauer garment and duffle bags.

Standard on all Explorer models are body-on-frame construction, rear anti-lock brakes, 19-gallon fuel tank, gas-pressurized shock absorbers, front and rear stabilizer bars, trailer tow rear step bumper and transfer case skid plates on four-wheel-drive models.

Size, Comfort and Style

With its 111.9-inch wheelbase and 184.3-inch overall length, the four-door Explorer is a large vehicle. However, it is very easy to drive, thanks to the commanding view from the driver's seat and the excellent visibility from the expansive greenhouse.

While it sits higher than conventional automobiles, the Explorer does not require a step ladder to climb into the cockpit. The Explorer's large doors and low step-in height make entry and exit an easy chore.

Once inside, the interior is huge. The rear seat area is inviting with its 60/40 split bench seat. The four-door Explorer's wheelbase is 9.8 inches longer than the two-door model and it is apparent that the gain is in rear seat room.

The ladder-type frame provides a solid foundation for the body and this solidness can be felt at speed. The Explorer's comfortable ride and on-the-road silence is equivalent to a full-size sedan. This sedan-like ride is a large part of Explorer's popularity.

Off the beaten path, the Explorer's generous travel suspension and 6.3-inch axle clearance absorbs ruts and bumps. During inclement weather and slippery conditions, activating the push button four-wheel drive adds even more comfort and security behind the wheel.

Jack Telnack's design group hit a home run with the Explorer. Ford designers were able to disguise the large and tall exterior of the Explorer by integrating extra large glass areas into the design. This expansive greenhouse gives the design a light and airy feeling. The two-tone exterior — with contrasting lower panel — visibly makes the vehicle seem much smaller than it actually is.

Gentle curves and the slightly flared fender wells make the Explorer much more than a two-box design. The Explorer's clean aerodynamics continue through to the roof racks which are sculpted like a pair of air spoilers.

ENGINE AND DRIVETRAIN

The Explorer is available with one engine that has two different horsepower ratings, depending on the transmission it is mated to. The 4.0-liter V-6 uses the latest generation of Ford's advanced EEC-IV computer-monitoring engine control system. EEC-IV monitors and constantly adjusts the engine's ignition timing, fuel mixture to optimize fuel economy and performance based on input parameters that include engine speed, engine temperature, altitude and load.

The multi-port, electronic fuel injected V-6 is rated at 145 horsepower at 3,800 rpm and 220 foot-pounds of torque at 2,400 rpm when teamed with the standard five-speed manual transmission. With the optional four-speed overdrive automatic, the numbers are 160 horsepower at 4,400 rpm and 225 foot-pounds of torque at 2,400 rpm.

While available with two-wheel drive, the majority of Explorers are outfitted with Ford's excellent four-wheel-drive system. The system features automatic-locking front hubs with a push button transfer case that permits on-the-fly shifting from two-wheel drive to four-wheel. This system is much slicker and easier than pulling a lever as required by many other systems. Shifting the Explorer into low-range four-wheel drive is done by push button, but does require a complete stop.

The Explorer powertrain, when matched up with the proper final drive ratio, makes it a strong tow vehicle. A properly equipped Explorer can tow up to 3,500 pounds with the standard rear step bumper. With aftermarket towing hitches and receivers, and Ford's optional towing package, a maximum trailer weight can reach 5,400 pounds on a two-wheel drive and 5,200 pounds, under four-wheel drive. Both the automatic and manual transmission models can be ordered with final drive ratios as low as 3.73:1 to maximize towing performance. Buyers interested in towing should opt for the automatic model which are rated for higher maximum towing weights.

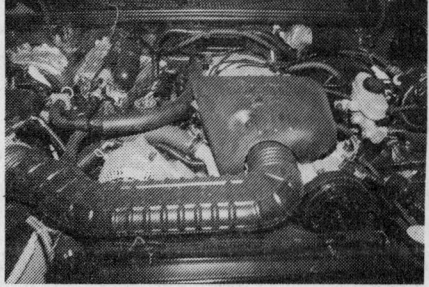

HANDLING

The handling of the Explorer is comparable to a passenger car during most maneuvers. However, when the turns get tighter and speeds increase, the Explorer's high-ground clearance and tall exterior forces it to lean more. This is partly due to the compromise in on- and off-road handling. The softly sprung chassis and large wheel travel are ideal for off-road driving and make for a passenger car-like ride on the freeway. However, in abrupt handling maneuvers this combination results in body roll.

This phenomenon is not unique to the Explorer. Nearly all sport utility vehicles with their higher ground clearance experience it. It should be noted that the Explorer has very safe, stable and predictable handling in 99.9 percent of all roadway situations. But it is a sport utility vehicle and like all sport utility vehicles, should not be driven like a sports car.

Brakes

Power front disc and rear drum brakes are standard on all models. The discs have a diameter of 10.28 inches. The rear drum diameter is 10 inches with a width of 2.5 inches. A rear-wheel anti-lock braking system also is standard on all Explorers. The ABS system is designed to reduce rear-wheel lock-up during severe braking applications regardless of weight differences over the rear axle. The Explorer stops from 60 mph in 150 feet.

Ride Quality

Much of the sale success of the Explorer can be attributed to its car-like ride quality. Ford engineers were able to achieve the remarkable by combining large wheel travel with relatively soft springing and gas-pressurized shock absorbers. The long 111.9-inch wheelbase also helps to smooth out the bumps and ruts.

On the highway, the Explorer's ride rivals a passenger car. Adding to the high quality is the quiet interior, made possible by the solid separate frame and body construction and clean aerodynamic lines that cut down on wind noise at speed.

INTERIOR

The term "car-like" comes up often when describing the various features of the Explorer. "Car-like" best describes the Explorer's large and inviting interior.

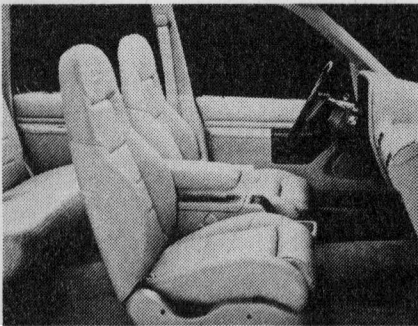

From the driver's point of view, the instrument panel is clear and easy to read. The dominant gauge is the speedometer, flanked by the tachometer and gauges registering the voltage, oil pressure, water temperature and fuel level. The center-mounted dash stereo system and climate controls are within easy reach.

The front reclining bucket seats are available in a knitted vinyl material on the XL and Sport models. Cloth reclining captain's chairs with a center console make up the XLT package and the top-of-the-line Eddie Bauer option adds an earthtone, mocha cloth to the XLT seating. The Eddie Bauer package also includes special trim and garment and duffle bags from the famous outfitter.

The spaciousness of the interior can be measured by the abundance of rear seat leg and headroom. The 60/40 rear bench seat allows one or both seat backs to be lowered to suit passenger- and cargo-carrying needs. With both seat backs lowered the cargo space grows to 81.6-cubic feet and can handle objects up to 72.9 inches in length.

SUMMARY

The Explorer's many car-like features and qualities cannot be matched by any of its sport utility competition. The Explorer's clean styling houses a huge interior that features comfortable seating that can be adjusted with its versatile fold-down rear seat backs to best suit passenger- and cargo-carrying needs.

Mechanically, the Explorer excels with its willing 4.0-liter V-6 engine and its shift-on-the-fly, push button four-wheel-drive transfer case. The suspension system is tuned for good on- and off-road manners.

The Explorer is solidly constructed and the quality of its fit-and-finish is very apparent throughout the exterior and interior.

1991 FORD EXPLORER XL

ASSETS	DEBITS
Huge passenger compartment	Excessive body roll
Anti-lock rear brakes	Could use more power for towing
Four-wheel-drive engaged with a push of a button	

HOW THE RUNNERS-UP PLACED FOLLOWING THE FORD EXPLORER XL

2nd PLACE...1991 Toyota Landcruiser

With 1991 restyling, Toyota went up market with the Landcruiser. The inline six is underpowered to haul 4,597 pounds. The Explorer's advantage is its interior and exterior styling and a better power-to-weight ratio.

3rd PLACE...1991 Chevrolet Suburban

Huge functional interior, but with little change from its mid-1960's inception, the design is showing its age. Complete remake of '92 model was long over due.

A CLOSER LOOK AT THE 1991 FORD EXPLORER XL

SPECIFICATIONS:	Front engine, four-wheel drive, four-door sport utility vehicle. A two-door version is available.
ENGINES:	V-6
DISPLACEMENT:	4.0 liter
HORSEPOWER:	160 @ 4,200 RPM
TORQUE:	225 foot-pounds @ 2,400 RPM
INDUCTION SYSTEM:	Electronic multi-port fuel injection
RECOMMENDED FUEL:	Unleaded regular
DRIVETRAIN:	Four-speed automatic
FRONT SUSPENSION:	Twin-traction beam axle, coil springs, gas-pressurized shock absorbers, stabilizer bar
REAR SUSPENSION:	Semi floating rear axle, two-stage leaf springs, gas-pressurized shock absorbers, stabilizer bar
STEERING TYPE:	Power-assisted recirculating ball-type
TURNING CIRCLE (CURB-TO-CURB):	35.6 feet
BRAKE TYPE:	Power-assisted front disc/rear drum with rear anti-lock
TIRE TYPE AND SIZE:	P225/70R15
WHEELBASE:	111.9 in.
LENGTH:	184.3 in.
WIDTH:	70.2 in.
HEIGHT:	67.3 in.
CURB WEIGHT:	4,046 pounds
TRUNK CARGO VOLUME:	42.6-cubic feet, 81.6-cubic feet with rear seat down
ACCELERATION, 0-60 MPH:	10.5 seconds
FUEL CONSUMPTION:	16-21 miles per gallon

BEST FULL-SIZE PICKUP TRUCK

The premium here is the ability to achieve passenger comfort, handling and ride while maintaining traditional full-size pickup traits of rugged reliability and large capacity towing and hauling.

THE CONTENDERS*	WHOLESALE	RETAIL
1988 Chevrolet C1500	$4,475	$5,400
1988 Dodge D100	$3,350	$4,250
1988 Ford F-150	$4,000	$4,900

*Prices of Contenders are base prices which may vary in range from those of the winning model.

The Winner

1988 CHEVROLET C1500 PICKUP

The full-size pickup truck is the workhorse of the automotive world. If you are serious about hauling or towing, a full-size pickup is the only answer. A big pickup has the grit to pull a horse trailer, lug fun toys like jetskis and motorcycles and take a load of garbage to the dump.

A grown-up pickup also is at home working five days a week on the farm, a construction site or transporting goods.

There are only three choices — all domestic — when it comes to selecting a full-size pickup. In the used pickup race, the Chevrolet C1500 outdistances its Dodge D100 and Ford F-150 rivals.

Contemporary pickups are also putting in lighter duty, never setting a tire off-road or having their beds loaded with dirty cargo. A golf bag might be the biggest payload handled by some pickups today.

The Big Three American automakers answered the demand for such "Cowboy Cadillacs" with creature comfort features and opulent options that rival passenger cars.

Rubber floor mats have been replaced with plush carpeting, and cloth bucket seats have become the norm over vinyl bench seats. The long list of options include power windows, door locks, cruise control, power steering, alloy wheels, premium sound systems and more.

Mechanically, the latest pickups have kept pace with the overhaul of the interior.

Larger versions — extended cabs and even four-door crew cabs — have further distanced late-model pickups from the trucks of old. Contemporary pickups are able to blend traditional workhorse traits with style and practicality that make them genuine alternatives to passenger cars.

The Chevrolet is the used pickup of choice as it was completely designed from the frame rails up and from the inside out in 1988. The 1988 Chevrolet, and its GMC Sierra twin, set a new standard among full-size pickups.

The 1986-91 Dodge and Ford models are essentially refinements from decades old designs. The Ford F-series received a facelift in 1992 and a new Dodge is scheduled for 1993.

The newer Chevrolet design is better able to meet the demands of the '90s truck owner. The exterior features the same 131.5-inch wheelbase as the previous model, but now boasts a longer, lower and more aerodynamic style. The exterior is 3-1/2 inches narrower, but the interior provides more leg and shoulder room and seat travel. The doors are larger, extending upward aircraft style into the roof line and downward nearly to the bottom of the rocker panel.

The larger doors, lower step-up height and high headroom make entry and exit much easier and greatly improve creature comfort.

The bed, or box is the working part of the truck. The Chevrolet tapes out at 49 inches between the wheel wells and nearly 64 inches between the side panels — wide enough to accommodate 5-foot wide building materials above the wheel wells.

The all-welded construction box has a seamless floor without bolts to improve corrosion resistance.

The ladder frame is a semi-perimeter design with a boxed front section making it especially sturdy in the front end where extra support is needed for the engine and front suspension. Robotic welding assures strength through precisely placed welds. The frame is hot-dip waxed to improve corrosion resistance.

The Chevrolet full-size pickup lineup includes the half-ton 1500 series, three-quarter ton 2500 series and one-ton 3500 series. In addition to the base two-wheel-drive C series, four-wheel-drive is available on K series versions. A longer wheelbase extended cab model with an optional folding bench seat for three is available on all models.

Three trim levels are available: Cheyenne, Scottsdale and Silverado.

Size, Comfort and Style

By having the latest makeover, the Chevrolet pickup took the lead in looks and style with its sleek (for a pickup) aerodynamic design. While the Dodge and Ford challengers feature traditional boxy exteriors, the Chevrolet is state-of-the-art sculpted design with its clean, shapely looks.

The new aero-look is carried out with flush side glass, modular-assembled, bonded-flush windshield, single-piece door frames and robotic welding. Hidden roof pillar and built-in drip rails eliminate matching problems on door cuts.

The top-of-the-line Silverado package is the most popular trim level for the

Chevrolet pickup. Other popular options include tilt, cruise, power windows and door locks, heavy-duty cooling, the 5.7-liter V-8 engine and automatic transmission.

The extended cab version, which has a value about $700 higher, with the "short" 6-1/2-foot bed is the most desirable Chevrolet pickup. The folding rear bench seat is perfect for children and can accommodate adults for short trips. There is no secret why the stretch cab is so popular, it makes the pickup that much more like a passenger car, while maintaining its utilitarian rear bed.

A sporty Sportside model features an updated version of the venerable stepside model. A four-wheel-drive Sportside model was selected "1988 Four Wheeler of the Year" by *Four Wheeler* magazine.

Unlike the uncompromising Ford twin-beam front axle, the Chevrolet has an independent coil spring front suspension with unequal length upper and lower control arms and shock absorbers mounted inside the coil springs.

The Chevrolet front suspension gives it the best ride in the pickup class. Used buyers should check if the previous owner had the factory "alignment kit" installed. The fix-it kit, approximately $150 installed, updates the 1988-91 models to the latest factory specifications.

ENGINE AND DRIVETRAIN

The heart of the Chevrolet full-size pickup is its strong lineup of powerplants which includes the venerable Chevrolet small-block V-8.

The standard engine is the 4.3-liter, Vortec V-6 with roller valve lifters for reduced friction. This rugged V-6 is based on the famous small-block V-8 and shares the same pistons, rods and many other parts with the 5.7-liter V-8.

Four optional V-8 engines are available — 5.0-liter, 5.7-liter, 6.2-liter diesel and 7.4-liter gas. All gasoline engines feature computer-controlled, throttle-body fuel injection for precise fuel control and fuel economy.

The various powerplants can be mated to three- and four-speed automatic transmissions with overdrive, or four- and five-speed manuals. A floor-mounted gear shift lever is standard with all manual transmissions.

The small-block Chevrolet V-8 has a well-earned reputation for reliability. It is not uncommon for owners to roll up 200,000 trouble-free miles with only oil and filter changes every 3,000 miles.

One of the most popular engine/transmission combinations is the 5.7-liter V-8 teamed with the four-speed automatic transmission. That powertrain when mated to a 3:42-to-1 final axle ratio provides excellent overall performance, from running downtown to towing a boat. Expect about 14 to 19 miles per gallon.

Pickup buyers looking for a little more economy, can opt for the V-6. A highly-recommended combination is the V-6, a five-speed manual and the 3:73-to-1 final axle ratio. The package is good for 20-22 miles per gallon and can tow up to 4,000 pounds.

Any of the engine combinations offer excellent underhood accessibility. The clean engine compartment also includes a serpentine drive belt, covered junction box, plastic brake fluid reservoir and aluminum master cylinder and radiator.

HANDLING

While it will never be a sports car, the Chevrolet pickup leads the full-size field in handling. The independent coil-spring front suspension is complemented by two-stage, multi-leaf rear springs.

The rear suspension features staggered rear shocks — one shock is mounted to the front of the rear axle and the other to the rear — which helps to reduce wheel hop.

Power steering is standard on all models. Parallelogram steering linkages are designed specifically for the independent front suspension. The steering gear system is mounted inside the frame rails for reduced turning diameter and better maneuverability.

Handling is predictable with the weight-bias front end having a tendency to understeer or plow into turns during quick maneuvers.

Brakes

Power front disc and rear drum brakes are standard on all models. A rear-wheel anti-lock braking system is also standard on all models. The ABS system is designed to reduce rear-wheel lock-up during severe braking applications regardless of weight differences over the rear axle. Pickups are most susceptible to rear-wheel lock-up when the bed is not, or lightly, loaded. From 60 miles per hour, the Chevrolet pickup stops in 145 feet, which is class-leading performance for a full-size pickup.

Ride Quality

The Chevrolet pickup will never be mistaken for a luxury car when it comes to ride quality. However, the long wheelbase does go a long way to smooth out the ride. The truck's solid construction also adds to the ride comfort.

Road noise and vibration are reduced by rubber-bushed cab mounts that help isolate road noise and reduce vibration. Like most pickups, the Chevrolet has a smoother highway ride when the cargo bed is filled to its weight capacity. The ride is nearly as smooth as a passenger car and just as quiet at highway speeds.

INTERIOR

There is plenty of room to stretch out in a Chevrolet pickup. The wide cab lends itself to a variety of seating layouts. The pickup takes on a sports car look with its optional bucket seats with console.

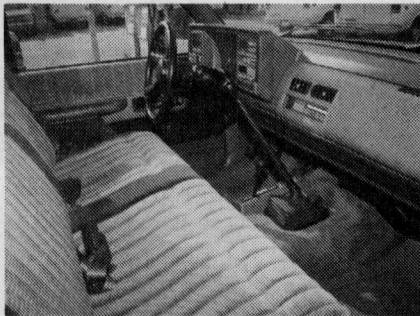

A more practical arrangement is the bench or 60/40 seats which easily allow three passengers to sit across the cab. Upholstery choices include vinyl or cloth. The cloth, which is more comfortable in hot and cold temperatures, is standard on the top-of-the-line Silverado.

Inside storage areas include a full-size glove box with cup holders, small bins in each door and a tight and narrow area behind the seats. Pickup buyers looking for more storage should take a serious look at the extended cab model with its dramatically increased storage area and fold-down jump seat for up to three occasional passengers. Without the rear seat, the extended cab adds 40.5 cubic feet of space for all kinds of gear.

Like General Motors' passenger cars, the Chevrolet pickup is blessed with GM's outstanding heating and cooling system. The heavy-duty heater includes side window defoggers. With even less interior volume to heat and cool, the pickup's climate control is even more impressive.

The instrument grouping consists of a high-tech cluster of round gauges. The speedometer is electrically driven for more accuracy.

SUMMARY

Chevrolet's C1500 beats its Dodge D100 and Ford F-150 competition because it was first to update its design. The newer design better appeals to the new truck buyer that is looking for an alternative to the traditional passenger car.

The consumer is also voting for the Chevrolet. With the new 1988 design, Chevrolet no longer automatically conceded the full-size pickup sales race to Ford.

In R.L. Polk registrations from Oct. 1, 1990 to Sept. 30, 1991, Chevrolet totaled 375,348 units, compared to 372,697 full-size Ford pickups. However, Ford claims it is still No.1 when fleet sales are added in.

No matter who is king of the full-size pickups, the fight for the title means good values and bargains for consumers.

This is where the buyer of a late-model used Chevrolet pickup has to be careful. With all the factory incentives, rebates and discount financing, overall, it can be cheaper to buy a new pickup, than a one-year old model.

1988 CHEVROLET C1500

ASSETS	DEBITS
New aerodynamic design	No headrests with bench seats
Anti-lock rear brakes	Wide 49 feet turning circle
Proven small-block V-8	Extended cab option

HOW THE RUNNERS-UP PLACED
FOLLOWING THE CHEVROLET C1500
2nd PLACE...The 1988 Ford F150

A proven workhorse that was overdue for its 1992 reskinning.

3rd PLACE...The 1988 Dodge D100
The most dated styling. However the powerful Cummings Turbo Diesel
is a definite plus.

A CLOSER LOOK AT THE 1988 CHEVROLET C1500

SPECIFICATIONS:	Front engine, two-wheel drive, two-door pickup truck. Options include four-wheel drive, extended cab and four-door crewcab versions.
ENGINE:	V-8
DISPLACEMENT:	5.7 liter
HORSEPOWER:	210 @ 4,000 RPM
TORQUE:	300 foot-pounds @ 2,800 RPM
INDUCTION SYSTEM:	Electronic fuel injection
RECOMMENDED FUEL:	Unleaded regular
DRIVETRAIN:	Three-speed automatic
FRONT SUSPENSION:	Independent with coil springs
REAR SUSPENSION:	Multi-leaf rear springs
STEERING TYPE:	Variable-ratio, power assisted
TURNING CIRCLE (CURB-TO-CURB):	49 feet
BRAKE TYPE:	Power-assisted front disc/rear drum
TIRE TYPE AND SIZE:	P205/75R15
WHEELBASE:	131.5 in.
LENGTH:	194.1 in.
WIDTH:	76.6 in.
HEIGHT:	70.4 in.
CURB WEIGHT:	3,665 pounds
TRUNK CARGO VOLUME:	6.5 foot bed
ACCELERATION, 0-60 MPH:	Approximately 9 seconds
FUEL CONSUMPTION:	Approximately 14-19 miles per gallon

BEST COMPACT PICKUP TRUCK

The premium here is the ability to achieve passenger comfort, handling and ride with reliability and traditional pickup utility.

THE CONTENDERS*	WHOLESALE	RETAIL
1989 Ford Ranger	$4,925	$5,850
1989 Nissan Hardbody	$4,075	$5,000
1989 Toyota Long Bed 6	$5,225	$6,175

*Prices of Contenders are base prices which may vary in range from those of the winning model.

The Winner

1989 TOYOTA PICKUP

Compact pickups have come a long way since they debuted on American shores in the late 1960s. These very simple vehicles soon proved they were more than a smaller version of the traditional workhorse pickup. Their low initial cost and miserly operating costs appealed not only to farmers and commercial users, but mainstream car buyers.

By the mid-1970s, the inexpensive and very practical compact pickup proved to be a viable alternative to economy cars. Compact pickups during the week could commute to work, run to the grocery store and go to school. On weekends the versatile pickup could move furniture, haul trash, tow a boat and go on fishing trips. The compact pickup was basic, reliable transportation and even more.

As the number of domestic uses for compact pickups grew, the vehicles evolved with more creature comforts and passenger car style equipment and options. With the domestic automakers entering the market in the '80s, the increased competition pushed compact pickups to new levels of comfort and performance.

Toyota has been a leader in the compact truck field and is the No.1 importer. The Toyota pickup is the best used compact pickup because no other brand can match its hard earned reputation for rugged construction and long-term reliability.

Worthy competing trucks include the Ford Ranger and the Nissan Hardbody; both solid vehicles, but still falling short to the Toyota when it comes to proven reliability.

Toyota pickup reliability is more than just advertising hype. The pickup's rugged construction and legendary reliability is confirmed by thousands of Toyota owners each month.

For the past three years, Toyota has been broadcasting television commercials that feature testimony from owners that have rolled up more than 100,000 miles on their Toyota pickups. The TV spots end with "If you have a 100,000-mile, 200,000-mile, 300,000-mile or bigger story to tell, call 1-800-THE-TRUCK."

And call they do. According to Don Cecconi, Advertising Manager-Trucks for Toyota Motor Sales, U.S.A., Inc., thousands of pickup owners call each month.

"We probably average somewhere around a low of 1,200 a month to a high of 7,000 a month," he said. Cecconi admits the variation is due to how often the advertisement is on the air.

He said callers are sent a survey to fill out and Toyota uses the information for demographics, marketing and possibly a commercial.

Based on the surveys, at 100,000 miles, a Toyota pickup is just getting broken in. Many of the survey participants have topped 200,000 miles and are still going strong.

Henry Waiters of Cloudcroft, New Mexico has the highest mileage Toyota pickup uncovered by the survey. Waiters had put 650,611 miles on his Toyota and even signed an affidavit to the fact.

The ability to withstand and endure 100,000-plus miles makes the Toyota pickup an outstanding value. The Toyota pickup placed first in the J.D. Power & Associates Light Duty Truck Customer Satisfaction Index for 1989. The popularity of the pickup and the economy of large production also has made replacement parts affordable from the factory and the aftermarket.

The '89 model is an excellent choice as Toyota completely redesigned the pickup that year with car-like interiors, a more rounded exterior design and introduced an available V-6 engine.

The trend toward more passenger car features include four new colors — cardinal red, medium brown metallic, desert tan and medium red pearl — the first pearlescent color available on a Toyota truck. The '89 model also featured increased use of galvannealed sheet metal to help reduce corrosion.

You can have your Toyota pickup eight ways — Standard Bed, Standard Bed Deluxe, Long Bed Deluxe, Long Bed SR5, Xtracab Deluxe, Xtracab SR5 V-6, One Ton and Cab Chassis. The standard two-wheel drive layout is complemented by optional four-wheel drive.

Size, Comfort and Style

Toyota took the opportunity of the '89 redesign to inch its pickup closer to being a practical car with an even more practical trunk — a pickup bed.

The new truck is quieter than the previous model due to additional reinforcement of the back panel, roof and pillars. For increased isolation, specially tuned mounts attach the cab to the frame. The front engine mount has been redesigned on the V-6, reducing engine vibration. A longer rear leaf spring gives a smoother ride over all kinds of terrain.

Ride comfort levels with a Toyota pickup is also a multiple choice. The Standard model rides on a 103-inch wheelbase and has the firmer ride common with base compact pickups. The ride is firm and improves with a load in the bed.

The Long Bed models benefit from a longer 112.2-inch wheelbase that helps to smooth out much of the harshness of the shorter wheelbase model. The still longer wheelbase — 121.5 inches — of the Xtracab models further enhances the ride comfort qualities. It is about $900 more than the Long Bed model.

Within the Long Bed and Xtracab models are Deluxe and SR5 trim levels. The Deluxe versions emphasize ride and sporty SR5 suspension settings lean toward firm handling.

With the '89 exterior makeover, Toyota rounded the corners to give the pickup a more aerodynamic look. The previous model's wheel well flares have been smoothed out. The Xtracab model features a bold "B" pillar window that greatly improves visibility.

The four-wheel-drive Toyota pickups boast a high ground clearance of 7.7 inches and 15-inch wheels and large P225/75R15 tires for the rugged off-road look. It adds about $900 to the price of the 2WD.

ENGINE AND DRIVETRAIN

Standard and manual transmission Deluxe level pickups are powered by a four-cylinder engine displacing 2.4 liters. The carbureted unit is rated at 103 horsepower at 4,800 rpm and 133 foot-pounds of torque at 2,800 rpm.

A better choice is the electronically fuel-injected version that has an output of 116 horsepower at 4,800 rpm and 140 foot-pounds of torque at 2,800 rpm. In addition to 12 percent more horsepower, the fuel injected pickup has better driveability, more response and instant starting in all weather conditions.

A new option for '89 is the electronically fuel-injected 3.0-liter engine that pumps out 150 horsepower at 4,800 rpm and 180 foot-pounds of torque at 3,400 rpm. The V-6 is standard on the SR5 V-6, One Ton and Cab Chassis and is optional on Deluxe Long Bend and Xtracab models.

The four-cylinder Toyota Pickup is good for 22 miles per gallon city and 26 mpg on the highway. The more powerful V-6 is rated at 19 city and 24 highway. The small sacrifice in fuel economy is worth the silky smoothness that no four cylinder can match.

The extra power of the V-6 also increased towing capacities to 3,500 pounds with automatic models and up to 5,000 pounds with the One Ton model. The One Ton also is rated for a 2,655 pound payload — heaviest of any truck in its class.

The base Standard Bed is only available with a four-speed manual transmission. All other models can be equipped with a five-speed manual transmission or a four-speed automatic.

The same transmission choices are available on four-wheel-drive models. New for '89 is the shift-on-the-fly, four-wheel-drive system that disengages the front propeller shaft, differential and driveshaft in two-wheel-drive mode, giving improved fuel economy and reducing noise and vibration. When four-wheel drive is engaged, a sliding sleeve connects the front driveshafts to the propeller shaft and differential, and allows for a smooth transition to four-wheel drive.

HANDLING

The basic Toyota Pickup models have handling very similar to other compact trucks. However, the gap between the Toyota and other pickups broadens with the SR5 model.

The SR5 designation runs throughout the Toyota passenger and truck line up and represents its sporty versions. The SR5 pickup is no different. Closer to a two-door coupe in handling than a pickup truck, the SR5 tightens up and retunes the suspension with stiffer shock absorbers, higher rate front torsion bars and rear leaf springs.

The SR5 is an excellent choice when you really want a sporty handling car, but need the utility of a little pickup.

The aftermarket is well stocked with accessories and components to lower the height of the compact pickups and bring handling to true sports car level.

Much of the components were developed from the Sports Car Club of America's professional pickup truck racing series.

On the other end of the handling scale are the four-wheel-drive Toyota Pickups. However, when compared to compact 4x4 competitors with less sophisticated suspensions, the Toyota has a definite edge. This is achieved by an independent front suspension with upper and lower A-frame arms, gas-filled shock absorbers and a stabilizer bar.

The rear suspension features a live axle controlled by leaf springs with staggered hydraulic shock absorbers that reduce axle windup and hop under hard usage.

The four-wheel-drive model, because of its higher ground clearance, understeers and exhibits much more body lean in quick maneuvers, but its handling is very predictable.

Brakes

Power front disc and rear drum brakes are standard on all models. The two-wheel-drive One Ton and Cab Chassis models also have a rear load-sensing proportioning valve. The proportioning valve reduces the amount of braking at the rear when the truck is lightly loaded and more prone to lock up the rear brakes and tires. The amount of rear braking is proportionally increased as the rear weight bias increases. The load-sensing proportioning valve is standard on all four-wheel-drive models.

In 1991, Toyota made computer-controlled, rear-wheel anti-lock braking optional on four-cylinder SR5 models and standard on the SR5 V-6.

Ride Quality

The ride quality of the '89 Toyota Pickup shows a marked improvement over the previous year. The improvement is the result of strengthening the body structure, mounting the cab to the frame with specially tuned mounts and optimizing the mounting and placement of the engine. Another '89 change that improved the ride quality was a longer rear spring that maintains the load-carrying capacity, but with more resiliency. Like most pickups, the Toyota Pickup has a smoother highway ride when the cargo bed is filled to its weight capacity. If a passenger car-like ride is a high priority, select a Toyota SR5 pickup model.

INTERIOR

The redesign of the '89 Toyota Pickup included an overhaul of the interior. The new interior features a rounded, cockpit-style dash. Most commonly used controls — such as windshield wipers and lights — are close at hand. The redesigned dash included moving the radio location upward and adding convenient cupholders.

The new interior also is larger than the previous year. The greatest gain is with the Xtracab models, which are now nine inches longer than before and feature forward-facing rear jump seats for occasional rear passengers. The rear seats feature three-point seat belts, and when not in use, fold up to reveal two covered storage bins.

Xtracab models also feature new flip-open rear quarter windows for improved ventilation, and available dark tinting on rear and quarter windows for security and reduced heat gain on sunny days.

Regular cab models are available with bench or bucket seats. The bench seat has center seat belts, but three-across adult seating is very tight and the stick or automatic shifter intrudes.

SUMMARY

The compact pickup may be the most practical of all vehicles. It's fun to drive and easy to maneuver, inexpensive to buy and own, and practical with a capital "P."

With any used vehicles, reliability and dependability are on the top of the list. This is where the Toyota Pickup shines over its rivals. The Toyota is first in the hearts of its owners and also the critical surveys of J.D. Power and Associates. Toyota Pickups have thousands of faithful followers that would drive nothing else. They call by the thousands each month to tell Toyota how tough their trucks are and how satisfied they are with the product. Testimony like that is hard to beat.

The Toyota, which was updated in 1989, has successfully made the transition from practical little truck to a vehicle that is as comfortable and economical to drive as a passenger car. The Toyota is the No. 1 imported pickup truck and as of 1991 were also being manufactured at Fremont, Calif.

1989 TOYOTA PICKUP

ASSETS
New V-6 power
Outstanding reliability
Extended cab option

DEBITS
Smaller than Ford Ranger

HOW THE RUNNERS-UP PLACED
FOLLOWING THE TOYOTA PICKUP

2nd PLACE...1989 Ford Ranger
Wide variety of engines and models offered including a roomy Supercab version.

3rd PLACE...1989 Nissan Hardbody
Hardbody design was introduced in 1986, redesign cycle behind Toyota, which was reworked in 1989. Features same basic package as Toyota, but with fewer variations.

A CLOSER LOOK AT THE 1989 TOYOTA PICKUP

SPECIFICATIONS:	Front engine, rear-wheel drive, two-door pickup truck. Options include four-wheel drive and extended cab versions.
ENGINE:	4 cylinder
DISPLACEMENT:	2.4 liter
HORSEPOWER:	116 @ 4,800 RPM
TORQUE:	140 foot-pounds @ 2,800 RPM
INDUCTION SYSTEM:	Electronic fuel injection
RECOMMENDED FUEL:	Unleaded regular
DRIVETRAIN:	Five-speed manual
FRONT SUSPENSION:	Independent with torsion bar
REAR SUSPENSION:	Multi-leaf rear springs

STEERING TYPE:	Recirculating ball
TURNING CIRCLE (CURB-TO-CURB):	36.1 feet
BRAKE TYPE:	Power-assisted front disc/rear drum
TIRE TYPE AND SIZE:	P195/75R14
WHEELBASE:	103.0 in.
LENGTH:	174.6 in.
WIDTH:	66.5 in.
HEIGHT:	60.8 in.
CURB WEIGHT:	2,760 pounds
TRUNK CARGO VOLUME:	75.0 inch bed
ACCELERATION, 0-60 MPH:	Approximately 12 seconds
FUEL CONSUMPTION:	Approximately 22-26 miles per gallon

BEST STATION WAGON

The criteria for the best station wagon has always been the same throughout the ages: the ability to transport a combination of passengers and cargo with the ease, comfort and style of a sedan.

THE CONTENDERS*	WHOLESALE	RETAIL
1989 Buick Electra Estate Wagon	$9,250	$10,650
1990 Ford Taurus Wagon LX	$7,450	$8,650
1987 Volvo 740 GLE Turbo Wagon	$8,025	$9,275

*Prices of Contenders are base prices which may vary in range from those of the winning model.

The Winner

1990 FORD TAURUS WAGON LX

Before the minivan, there was the station wagon. While the minivan has displaced the station wagon as the traditional family hauler in recent years, there is still a definite niche for station wagons.

In fact, the family wagon could be making a comeback. Buick recently brought back its Roadmaster Estate Wagon and Volvo has launched an aggressive advertising campaign claiming a station wagon is safer than a minivan in an accident.

The 1948 Ford Super Deluxe Woodie Wagon and its contemporaries like the classy Chrysler Town & Country Wagon, established what a passenger station wagon was all about. A proper station wagon did not sacrifice any passenger car comfort or style, but was able to haul the entire family and the family dog to visit Aunt Ruby on Sunday afternoon.

More than 40 years later, a station wagon's duties have changed little. Real wood siding may be out, but today's station wagons are continuing to serve families faithfully.

Current station wagons are still based on and produced off of sedan platforms. Some spinoffs work and look better than others. The 1990 Ford Taurus Wagon LX is the best station wagon because it is a fully integrated package that is as good as the sedan it is based on.

The Taurus Wagon, available in L, GL and LX trim packages, continues the aerodynamic theme of the Taurus sedan. The Taurus Wagon and its Mercury Sable twin are built on the same 106-inch wheelbase, front-wheel-drive platform as their sedan counterparts. At 192 inches the Wagon is four inches longer in overall length than the sedan.

The Taurus Wagon and sedan are basically mechanically identical, except for the rear suspension design. The sedan uses a MacPherson strut design and the Wagon uses a torsion beam that allows it to carry up to a 1,200-pound load.

The clean aerodynamic lines of the sedan transfer well to the Wagon. The sedan has a drag coefficient of 0.32, with the Wagon coming in at 0.36 — excellent for a station wagon.

When the Taurus debuted in 1986 it represented a $3 billion gamble by Ford that the public would buy "jellybean" shaped front-wheel-drive family cars. Ford won that bet which led to Taurus becoming one of the top-selling cars in the nation, with earnings topping General Motors and designer Jack Telnack being made a Ford vice president. The new, aerodynamic Taurus represented the very best in domestic design and sophistication back in 1986.

The Taurus wagon can be outfitted with a variety of seating arrangements for five to eight passengers. The middle model GL is well equipped and includes the 3.0-liter V-6, four-speed overdrive automatic transmission, power steering, dual power outside mirrors, intermittent wipers, tinted glass, tilt steering column and stereo radio.

The XL adds many options as standard including air conditioning, power windows, power door locks, power driver's seat, speed control, rear-window defroster, bucket seats, center console, clearcoat paint, light group and cassette player. A popular option is the rear-facing third seat.

Taurus received a facelift for the 1992 model year. The $615 million investment by Ford was to freshen up the exterior and refine the package in the areas of noise, vibration, harshness and structural rigidity. The interior also benefitted from a complete makeover.

However, Ford was very conservative with the exterior styling changes. Since the Taurus is its big seller — "if it's not broken, don't fix it." By not wanting to depart too much from the original styling, the differences are only noticeable if the old and new cars are parked side-by-side. This is a blessing for the used car buyer, as his pre-1992 Taurus still looks like the latest model and has not gone the way of planned obsolescence.

Size, Comfort and Style

The Taurus Wagon has a 106-inch wheelbase and an overall length of 192 inches. With just four additional inches in length, the Wagon is as nimble and maneuverable as the sedan model. It can be parked in spots that traditional, full-size station wagons have to pass up.

The wagon's back design dedicates approximately 75 percent of the length to the passenger compartment. Front seat room and comfort is very good, and again identical to the highly-rated sedan. The front passenger area can be ordered with a split bench seat for three across seating, or with bucket seats. The back bench seat has room for three adult passengers with a bit more headroom.

The Taurus' award-winning styling was penned by Jack Telnack's design group at Ford and pioneered the domestic trend toward aerodynamic styling. Actually the Wagon carries out this theme more so than the sedan, with its roofline gently sloping to the aerodynamically sound rear treatment. This aero theme can also be seen in the roof rack which is designed with smooth edges to cut through the air.

The exterior of the Wagon is light and airy with its thin pillars and large expanses of glass. The large greenhouse also makes for great visibility from the driver's seat. The Taurus Wagon's styling has aged well.

ENGINE AND DRIVETRAIN

The base engine with the Wagon is a 3.0-liter V-6 that is rated at 140 horsepower at 4,800 rpm and 160 foot-pounds at 3,000 rpm. The pushrod engine has electronic multiport fuel injection and runs on unleaded regular gasoline. The 3.0-liter unit is a popular powerplant throughout the Ford fleet, seeing duty in the Tempo compact, Ford Ranger pickup and Probe sports coupe. In the Wagon, the EPA mileage rating is 20 miles per gallon city and 29 mpg highway.

The optional engine on the Wagon displaces 3.8-liters and also produces 140 horsepower. However, the larger engine's horsepower is developed at just 3,800 rpm. More importantly, the electronic, multiport, fuel injected engine generates 215 foot-pounds of torque — 55 more than the 3.0-liter version — at a very low 2,200 rpm. The 3.8-liter unit is EPA rated at 18 mpg city and 28 mpg highway.

The added low-end power of the larger engine can definitely be felt behind the wheel. Just tipping the throttle gets the engine into its powerband and the Wagon instantly responds. The small sacrifice in fuel economy is a good tradeoff for the gain in performance. The larger engine is the choice, particularly if the Wagon is used at or near its capacity.

The four-speed automatic transmission with overdrive shifts smoothly and positively. The Taurus' well-developed chassis does a good job in putting the front-wheel-drive power to the road. There is no shutter and torque steer under hard acceleration as with many front-wheel-drive autos. This is not surprising since the same basic suspension handles the 220-horsepower of the high-performance Taurus SHO.

The front-wheel-drive Wagon has a big advantage over conventional rear-wheel-drive station wagons when it comes to a slippery surface or inclement weather. The engine and transaxle weight over the driving tires dramatically increases traction, when compared to rear-wheel drive.

The Wagon is rated to tow up to a 2,000-pound trailer and Ford offers optional special towing packages.

HANDLING

The Taurus Wagon is surprisingly nimble and handles easily for a station wagon. This is because the basic chassis and suspension only slightly differs from the Taurus sedan.

When the Taurus was initially being developed, three-time world driving champion Jackie Stewart did much of the testing and handling development. By the time Stewart was satisfied, he had set a new track record at Ford's Detroit testing grounds. The record formerly was held by a 5.0-liter Mustang.

Stewart's work translates into a station wagon that handles like no other domestic station wagon. The Wagon is responsive and exhibits little body roll in corners. It is fun to drive.

The front suspension is independent with MacPherson struts, coil springs, gas-pressurized shocks, and an anti-roll bar. The rear suspension utilizes a torsion beam, SLA independent suspension with coil springs, gas-pressurized shock absorbers, and an anti-roll bar.

Brakes

Power front disc and rear drum brakes are standard on the Wagon. The front disc diameter is 10 inches, with a rear drum diameter of 9.8 inches. From 60 miles per hour, the Wagon stops in 143 feet. An anti-lock braking system is optional on the 1992 models.

Ride Quality

The Wagon's fully independent suspension and gas-pressurized shock absorbers do well in handling bumps and rough surfaces. The ride of the Wagon is not adversely affected when it is filled to capacity with passengers or cargo.

The ride quality is also enhanced by the low wind noise at highway speeds, due to the Wagon's clean aerodynamics.

INTERIOR

The interior of the Wagon is available with a pair of front bucket seats, or a 50/50 split bench seat that can sit two adults and a child in the center position. The three across seating would be tight for three adults.

Practically any size driver can find a comfortable position behind the wheel of the Wagon. If you can find one, the optional six-way power seat is recommended.

The dash panel is easy to see through the two-spoke steering wheel. The dash layout places the instrument panel and other controls directly in front of the driver. The optional cruise control is conveniently located in the steering wheel hub.

The rear 60/40 split bench seat offers adequate room for three adults. To handle long loads or bulky cargo, one or both of the rear seat sections can fold flat and flush with the cargo floor. The optional rear-facing third seat allows the Wagon to carry up to eight passengers. However, three of the eight passengers would have to be children — one for the center front bench and two for the third seat. A Driver's side airbag became available in 1991 and driver's side and passenger airbags are available on the '92 model.

SUMMARY

The 1990 Ford Taurus Wagon LX is the best used station wagon because it is does not deviate much from the award-winning sedan it is based on. The Taurus Wagon also is very maneuverable and easy to drive and park, when compared to much larger conventional station wagons. The front-wheel-drive layout maximizes passenger and cargo space, while giving it exceptional traction in loose and slippery conditions. The recent, mild facelift of the '92 model ensures the '90 Taurus will still look fresh and new in the years ahead.

1990 FORD TAURUS WAGON LX

ASSETS
Aerodynamic design
Handling is great for a Wagon
Engine performance

DEBITS
Front bench seat is
tight for three adults

HOW THE RUNNERS-UP PLACED
FOLLOWING THE FORD TAURUS WAGON LX

2nd PLACE... 1989 Buick Electra Estate Wagon
A traditional rear-wheel-drive wagon that lacks the style, handling and driveability of the Taurus Wagon.

3rd PLACE... 1987 Volvo 740 GLE Turbo Wagon
Even when turbocharged, the 740's four-cylinder lacks the smooth and wide powerband of power from the Taurus' V-6.

A CLOSER LOOK AT THE 1990 FORD TAURUS WAGON LX

SPECIFICATIONS:	Front engine, front-wheel drive, four-door station wagon.
ENGINE:	V-6
DISPLACEMENT:	3.0 liter
HORSEPOWER:	140 @ 4,800 RPM
TORQUE:	160 foot-pounds @ 3,000 RPM
INDUCTION SYSTEM:	Electronic multipoint fuel injection
RECOMMENDED FUEL:	Unleaded regular
DRIVETRAIN:	Four-speed automatic
FRONT SUSPENSION:	Independent with coil springs, gas-pressurized shocks, anti-roll bar
REAR SUSPENSION:	SLA independent with coil springs, gas-pressurized shock absorbers, anti-roll bar
STEERING TYPE:	Power assisted rack-and-pinion
TURNING CIRCLE (CURB-TO-CURB):	41 feet

BRAKE TYPE: Power-assisted front disc/rear drum
TIRE TYPE AND SIZE: P205/70R14
WHEELBASE: 106.1 in.
LENGTH: 192.0 in.
WIDTH: 71.2 in.
HEIGHT: 54.1 in.
CURB WEIGHT: 3,375 pounds
ACCELERATION, 0-60 MPH: 11 seconds
FUEL CONSUMPTION: 20-29 miles per gallon

Subscription Options for 1992

Get a complete picture of the 1992 automotive market

A
USED CAR PRICES — This 1 year subscription includes four updated versions of USED CAR PRICES.
Domestic: (includes bulk rate shipping & handling) $21.95
Other Countries: (includes air mail shipping & handling) $29.95

B
NEW VEHICLE PRICES — This 1 year subscription covers the complete automotive market of new vehicles for a total of 9 books: three NEW CAR (Domestic); two IMPORT CAR; three VAN, PICKUP, SPORT UTILITY; and one ECONOMY CAR.
Domestic: (includes bulk rate shipping & handling) $46.95
Other Countries: (includes air mail shipping & handling) $66.95

C
NEW and USED CAR PRICES — This 1 year subscription includes: three NEW (Domestic); four USED CAR; and two IMPORT CAR - for a total of 9 books.
Domestic: (includes bulk rate shipping & handling) $46.95
Other Countries: (includes air mail shipping & handling) $66.95

D
PREMIUM SUBSCRIPTION — *Exciting New Offer for 1992.*
This 1 year subscription offers our full-line of books *PLUS* a *Free* copy of our *New* ULTIMATE OWNER'S MANUAL (an $8.95 value). The total of 14 books includes: three NEW CAR (Domestic); four USED CAR; two IMPORT CAR; three VAN, PICKUP, SPORT UTILITY; one ECONOMY CAR; and the *Free* ULTIMATE OWNER'S MANUAL all at a substanial savings to you.
Domestic: (includes bulk rate shipping & handling) $65.95
Other Countries: (includes air mail shipping & handling) $99.95

SCHEDULED RELEASE DATES FOR 1992
(Prices accurate thru cover date)

VOL. 26 (1992)		Release Date	Cover Date
U2601	USED CAR PRICES	Dec. '91	April '92
N2601	NEW CAR PRICES (Domestic)	Jan. '92	June '92
S2601	VAN, PICKUP, SPORT UTILITY BUYER'S GUIDE . .	Jan. '92	June '92
I2601	IMPORT CAR PRICES	Feb. '92	July '92
E2601	ECONOMY CAR BUYER'S GUIDE	Feb. '92	1992
U2602	USED CAR PRICES	Mar. '92	July '92
N2602	NEW CAR PRICES (Domestic)	May '92	Nov. '92
S2602	VAN, PICKUP, SPORT UTILITY BUYER'S GUIDE . .	May '92	Nov. '92
U2603	USED CAR PRICES	June '92	Oct. '92
I2602	IMPORT CAR PRICES	June '92	Dec. '92
U2604	USED CAR PRICES	Sept. '92	Jan. '93
N2603	NEW CAR PRICES (Domestic 1993)	Nov. '92	Feb. '93
S2603	VAN, PICKUP, SPORT UTILITY BUYER'S GUIDE . .	Nov. '92	Feb. '93

PLUS NEW 1992 PUBLICATIONS

O2601	ULTIMATE OWNER'S MANUAL	1992
A2601	AMERICAN DREAM CAR	1992
CG2601	IMPORT CAR COLLECTOR'S GUIDE	1992
BN2601	20 BEST NEW CARS	1992
BU2601	20 BEST USED CARS	1992

Your Order Form: Mail Today! With your Check, Money Order, MasterCard or VISA

SUBSCRIPTIONS

For descriptions of Subscription Packages, see inside back cover.

Check box next to your selection. Please enclose payment with your order.

A ☐ **Used Car Prices** 4 books per year .... $ 21.95

B ☐ **New Vehicle Prices** 9 books per year 46.95

C ☐ **New and Used Car Prices** 9 books per year 46.95

D ☐ **Premium Subscription** 14 books per year 65.95
Includes a FREE issue of Ultimate Owner's Manual (an $8.95 value)

SINGLE COPIES

Check box next to your selection. Please enclose payment with your order.

(Price shown includes $4.95 cover price plus $2.00 First Class shipping & handling per book.)

☐ **Used Car Prices** .... $ 6.95

☐ **New Car Prices** 6.95

☐ **Van, Pickup, Sport Utility Buyer's Guide** 6.95

☐ **Import Car Prices** 6.95

☐ **Economy Car Buying Guide** 6.95

Exciting New Annual Publications Available For 1992

☐ **Ultimate Owner's Manual**
$8.95 cover price plus shipping & handling .... $ 10.95

☐ **American Dream Cars**
$8.95 cover price plus shipping & handling 10.95

☐ **Import Car Collector's Guide**
$19.95 cover price plus shipping & handling 21.95

☐ **20 Best 1992 Cars, Vans & Trucks**
$5.95 cover price plus shipping & handling 7.95

☐ **20 Best Used Cars, Vans & Trucks 1986 - 1991**
$5.95 cover price plus shipping & handling 7.95

NOTE: Prices shown above are for shipping within the U.S. and Canada only. Other countries - **ADD $5.00** to the cover price per book (via air mail) and **$2.00** to the cover price per book (surface mail). **Please pay through American bank or with American currency.** (For subscription rates in other countries, see inside back cover.) Rates subject to change without notice.

☐ *I enclose check or money order for $*_____

☐ *I prefer to use my* ☐ **MASTER CARD** ☐ **VISA**   *Total Payment $*_____

Account # _____ Exp. Date _____

Signature _____

Name _____ Phone (_____)_____

Address _____

City _____ State _____ Zip _____

Please mail to: Edmund Publications Corp., Dept. BU2601, 200 Baker Ave., Concord, MA 01742-2112

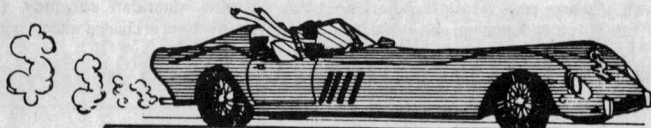